BECAUSE OF 4

A true story and step-by-step guide to uncovering
potential in youth and you.

CHERYL PETERSON, PH.D.

explore
ideas
PUBLISHING

Published by: Explore-IDEAS Publishing and imprint of Dr. Cheryl Peterson

Image Copyright © 2019 by Mackenzie Murray. mackenzie-murray.com

Photos Copyright © 2022 by Aaron Gang. aarongangphotography.pixieset.com

Paperback ISBN: 978-1-7377630-2-4

Hardcover ISBN: 978-1-7377630-5-5

Ebook ISBN: 978-1-7377630-3-1

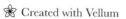 Created with Vellum

explore
iDeas
PUBLISHING

*Dedicated to 4 students
who allowed me to be their teacher
and taught me the importance of
play, practice and purpose.*

Contents

Letter from the Author   vii

Foreword   ix

Introduction   xi

Prologue   1

1. STUDENTS   3
   LEAN IN!

2. MIRACLES   13
   BELIEVE IN MIRACLES

3. HABITS   23
   THIRST FOR LEARNING

4. MINUTES   33
   BE IN THE MOMENT

5. SCHOLARS   45
   WHAT'S YOUR WORD?

6. LETTERS   55
   IT'S PLAYTIME!

7. IDEAS   69
   CHANGE THE WORLD

8. LEADERS   83
   Leap and Lead

9. PLANS   95
   Dream Big

10. HOUSES   109
    Build a Foundation

11. WEEKS   121
    Be Gritty!

12. GOOD-BYES   133
    GOOD...BYE

13. WORDS   145
    Make a Difference

14. PROMISES   155
    Tell Your Story

Afterword   169
Bibliography   171
Notes   175
Acknowledgments   183
About the Author   187
Also by Cheryl Peterson, Ph.D.   189

Letter from the Author

Dear teacher, parent, and coach,

I know you. I am you. I have worked alongside you. Our struggles and celebrations may be different, but in many ways, they are the same. This story, my journey, began amid personal crises. My whole world was crashing. It wasn't a major catastrophe, but large enough to fully disrupt my life. I'm sure you can relate. I wasn't sure how I would manage. But instead of merely surviving, I began to soar. It happened because of four.

BECAUSE OF 4 students, I learned the power of hope and love. Hope and love pulled me through my own dark place and inspired me to shine a light for four students who desperately needed it. In doing so I gained more than I gave. It wasn't easy, but in many ways, it was quite simple.

It's taken me a few years to get this story out. In that time, it feels as if the whole world has been turned upside down again. But I think this story may be a beacon of light so many are looking for right now. I hope the lessons I learned along my path inspire you and lead you to discover your own hope and love.

BECAUSE OF 4, I learned to stop trying to do more and start trying to be more of who I was meant to be and to encourage my students to do the same.

I invite you to come along with me, step-by-step, through this guide. Each chapter in this book begins with a provocation in which I share with you my story as I remember it. These provocations are followed by three sections: play, practice and purpose. In these sections I play with ideas related to the provocation, explore ways to put the ideas into practice, and present prompts to help you think deeper about your purpose. Each chapter concludes with a step-by-step worksheet to guide you in the theme of chapter with play, practice and purpose. Some chapters also have a create activity to inspire you to create a practice related to the book. For a free downloadable pdf of these worksheets, visit my website at drcherylpeterson.com. Also, look for my *Because of 4 Step-by-Step Workbook and Reflection Guide* on Amazon.

Thank you for reading. I hope this story is as inspiring for you as it was for me.

Cheryl Peterson, Ph.D.

Foreword

In a world of hustle and bustle, we are continuously on the go, never stopping to reflect. Often, we forget the importance of relationship building, the power of play, the necessity of practice, and discovering one's purpose, which all lead to deepened experiences. We simply follow along with the status quo, as the world passes us by, and time keeps on ticking. *Because of 4* is not another status quo book; it truly will take you on a journey.

Because of 4 shares the journey of four amazing boys and how Dr. Peterson created opportunities for them to play, practice, and discover their purpose, while inspiring the reader to do the same.

I hope you not only find the time to read but truly take time to dig into the story *Because of 4*. Dr. Peterson brings to life the importance of relationship building with her wonderful storytelling. She will help you create valuable learning experiences for yourself and others in your life, through the exercises and knowledge she shares within the pages of this book. I know my experience working with her, as well as reading the book, creating these valuable lessons for me, and I will be forever grateful.

So, Dr. P, I am so glad you put the words to paper and cannot wait for others to experience the power of *Because of 4*. The rest of you turn the page and get to the really good stuff!

With Love,

Mrs. G.

Introduction

I sat in the auditorium surrounded by teachers. It was our annual welcome back to school workshop. Everyone was excited to see each other and begin a new year. I was excited about my new role as gifted coordinator, but I also had a heavy weight on my shoulder. I tried to smile and focus on our guest speaker, Manny Scott, one of the original Freedom Writers[1]. The Freedom Writers was a name given to a group of students who wrote a book, *The Freedom Writers Diary*[2], with the guidance of their teacher, Erin Gruwell. This later became the name of a film starring Hilary Swank who played Gruwell, the tough inner-city teacher who made a difference by believing in her students and going the extra mile. Manny Scott shared a powerful story of how Ms. Gruwell changed his trajectory in life and how he used what he learned to build the life of his dreams.

I wanted to be that kind of teacher. I wanted to make a difference. I wanted to love my life. I wanted to love teaching. But quite honestly, right at that moment, at that season in my life, I felt a little used up. Challenges at home and with my job were taking just about every ounce of energy I had left. I wanted to go the extra mile, but I really didn't think I could even take the next step.

If you teach in any capacity whether it's in a school, as a coach on the field, or as a parent at home, you are going to have a day and probably more when it is difficult. Really difficult. You are going to have one of those days when you wonder what to do next and if it's all worth it. You are going to question yourself, your motives and even your own abilities. It might not even be the students making you feel this way. It might be the mess in your kitchen, the unfolded pile of laundry, the sore shoulder, lack of sleep, the quarrel with a friend or the latest news report pushing you to a point where you just can't breathe. On these days it is often difficult to take the next step. But sometimes a difficult day reveals what needs to change and pushes you to want more.

————

As I listened to Manny Scott, I knew I wanted more. I wanted to be more for myself, my family, and my students. I wanted an easy button. I wanted to breathe easier. I wanted everything to be easier. I whispered a silent prayer. The response I received was unexpected. Instead of getting easier, I got more. Four students more. These four students challenged me in many ways. They took time, energy, and emotion I didn't have to give. I struggled. I cried. Each day I took another breath and tried, again.

Over time, teaching them became more important than my own worries. As I struggled to figure out how to teach them, I became more aware of who I was and what I could do. I began to focus less on deficits and more on abundance. It wasn't the easy button, but in some ways it was making my life easier. I knew I couldn't give up. I knew I was doing something important. I could feel the change happening. I was becoming more of who I wanted to be, a better person, a better teacher, and even a better parent and coach.

Because of four students, I realized how to really connect with students and help them reach their potential. It's not about doing more. It's being more. *Because of 4* became my rally cry, my call to action, my purpose. It kept me going even when the challenges seemed stacked against me. Four students needed me at my best. In striving to be more, I gave and received more than I ever dreamed possible.

I originally wrote this story to capture and process my emotions and hold on to the moment. As I wrote, I realized this story wasn't just for me. It's for you, too. I want to inspire you to reflect on your own one, two, three, four or more students. You know the ones. The ones who need more than you can give. The ones you cry for on your way home from work. The ones you buy a winter coat for or put food in their backpacks on Friday, so they have something to eat over the weekend. The ones you are afraid you can't teach, but capture your heart when they light up with a love of learning for the first time. Maybe even the ones in your own home who exhaust you, frustrate you, and challenge you and yet are the ones for whom you would do almost anything.

That's why I decided to share this story. Somewhere out there are four students who will touch your heart. When one of these students walks into your classroom, sits at your dinner table or plays on your team, I want you to make a difference. I want you to see in them what I saw. I want you to uncover even more of their potential. I want you to be more for them and for you.

———

I believe within the ordinary stories of our lives are extraordinary moments; answers to our silently whispered prayers. These moments challenge us and push us to grow. They give us glimpses into our potential and allow us to be more than we ever thought possible. I want to take you step-by-step through these moments of my story and show you how to play with the ideas, suggest practices for uncovering potential and challenge you to discover your own story and purpose so you can be more…. **BECAUSE OF 4.**

Prologue

"WHATCHA DOIN IN HERE?"

"Why are you teaching us?"

I sighed, hiding my disappointment with a smile. I had been moving from classroom to classroom all day teaching enrichment lessons. Third grade was one of my favorites and I was hoping to find students with a spark, not dynamite. "I'm here looking for some good thinkers for my groups," I responded enthusiastically.

As the gifted specialist, I was trying a new approach to identifying students to participate in critical and creative thinking groups. I was teaching every student in every classroom. While I was teaching the teachers were watching and recording what they noticed.

The lessons were designed to be fun and engaging. I had already taught the lesson in several classrooms and was encouraged by the number of students who demonstrated creative and innovative ideas. The teachers commented on how they saw students engaging in ways they had never seen before. They had a new perspective of their students. But this room had a different energy. As I began teaching, rather than enjoying the lesson, I felt myself taking a deep breath and bracing my shoulders.

"I can't do this!" Michael shouted. He glared at me. "You won't take me. I'm stupid. I can't read."

Challenge accepted, I thought, holding his gaze. The atmosphere in the room was explosive. Little did I know this one moment would spark a change impacting my life and view of teaching forever.

———

I HAVE TAUGHT elementary school and gifted learners for many years and have been fortunate to have had wonderful experiences. Every year there are multiple students who offer new insight into my career, create new pathways or learning, and genuinely touch my heart; but until this year I have never felt like I made a difference.

That is, until the four; because of these four boys, I now know why I became a teacher. These four challenged my thinking and forced me outside of my comfort zone, beyond the daily description of my job, to a place where I was moved to discover what is truly possible when you give a little more than what is expected. Come along with me and meet the four, who I hope will impact you as much as they have impacted me.

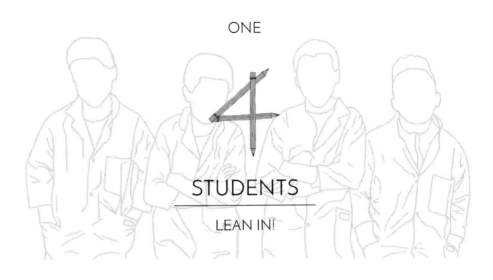

ONE

STUDENTS

LEAN IN!

The world is desperate for braver leaders. It's time for all of us to step up. -Brené Brown[1]

"YOU'VE GOT some tough kiddos in your class," I remarked to Mrs. G, passing by her third grade classroom before school. "I think I better take Michael for a small group to do some puzzles or something. I told him I would, if he worked hard while I was in there doing my lesson. I honestly wasn't sure I'd get through the lesson with this group. They took a ton of energy."

I DIDN'T KNOW Mrs. G very well yet. She was a new teacher in our building. I was serving a new role as gifted coordinator while also fulfilling my previous role as a gifted specialist. My role as gifted specialist included working in classrooms with small groups of students and coaching teachers. I was using this opportunity to get to know her better. When I was in her classroom the previous day, it

3

was chaos. There was a substitute teacher in her place, so I wasn't sure if that was the cause of the behavior I witnessed. I was curious about Mrs. G and her teaching style. I hoped to learn a little more about her and the class.

The reaction from third graders in her classroom was unusual. It was only the second week of school, typically a honeymoon period where students are fairly engaged and compliant. Students in other classes had enjoyed the lessons. This class was different. The students were not interested in me nor what I had to offer. A few confronted me saying I wasn't their teacher and they didn't have to listen to me. Not knowing the students only compounded the challenge.

One student, Michael, was particularly confrontational. He refused to even try the activities. He had a need to move and talk and continued to argue with me that he was stupid, and I would not take him anyway. I tried my best to connect with him by engaging in conversation about puzzles. He seemed interested and I suggested we could find a time for him to come to my classroom to try some. I promised he could work with me if he completed the activity. Time had moved slowly in this classroom. As I wrapped up my lesson and exited the classroom, a long, slow exhale of relief passed my lips.

———

AS I TALKED with Mrs. G about creating an extra group for Michael, I secretly hoped she would confirm it probably wasn't the best idea. I soon discovered she was not that kind of a teacher. She's not the kind to sit back and wait for good things to happen for kids, hoping someone will take care of them. She is the type of teacher who pushes everyone to do what is right for kids and makes things happen. She was about to push me.

"Yep, they're my lovelies. Michael keeps talking about you taking him. I think I have four boys you could pull for a group."

Four? I thought groaning silently. Smiling politely, I responded, "I'll see what I can find in my schedule. I really don't have a lot of time, and my groups are full, but I want to follow through on my promise to Michael to meet with me to do some puzzles." It wasn't much of a promise, but it worked, and I felt resolved to keep it.

––––––

MRS. G HANDED me a sheet of paper with four names on it. I immediately recognized two of the names belonging to boys I had seen in the cafeteria that morning. I had witnessed their unique leadership ability firsthand. Our school serviced students in kindergarten to third grade. Many of our students qualified for a free breakfast, filling the cafeteria with young, hungry bodies each morning.

As I was working breakfast in the cafeteria, two of the boys on the list, Larry and Rick came strutting in with Michael. Even though they were only third graders, every adult in the room watched them with high alert. The kids watched them too, some in awe and others in fear. The boys took it all in and worked the crowd.

"Oh yeah, I've seen Larry and Rick in action. They are talented leaders. They've got the whole school running around trying to figure out what to do with them. Imagine if we could channel that energy."

"I know, right," agreed Mrs. G with a lighthearted chuckle. "I'm also trying to start a mentor program to help them build some positive relationships. I think they would really like coming with you and it would be a positive thing."

"I'm not sure I know James," I said referring to the fourth boy on the list.

"James has something special; you need to meet with him too."

––––––

WHY DO *I offer these things? I can't do this.* I was so excited about my promotion from gifted specialist to coordinator, but the new role was adding responsibilities and tasks which dictated much of my time and calendar. I was supposed to be focused more on the overall district goals and administration of the program, but I also felt drawn to working directly with students. As if that wasn't stressful enough, my husband accepted a job out of state. I hadn't even told anyone yet. I wanted this job so badly. I just wanted a chance to do it well and I did not want to be focused on my end date.

My thoughts and fears continued to spin out of control. *I don't have time for this!* I screamed silently in my head. Yet, somewhere deep down, I knew the right thing to do was to support these boys. Within a few days, I found a thirty-minute opening in my schedule. *I can take the boys on Monday from 11:30-12:00. Will that work?* I e-mailed, leaning into the growth opportunity for the four boys...**and me.**

PLAY - Lean In!

When I was young my family and I stayed at a small resort for a week every summer. My memories of that time are filled with moments of play. During the day we created games, played catch or fished. At night we would play card or board games or make up shows for the family. There was also a beach where I would spend hours playing in the sand. Next to the beach was a large oak tree where I would swing. My cousins and I would try to see if we could touch the leaves and then see who could jump the farthest into the sand. The beach provided a sandbox full of opportunity to create castles, sculptures or sand drawings.

Throughout my childhood, one of my favorite playgrounds was the sandbox. In a sandbox I could sift sand, fill things, and dump things out. I could create things or just move sand and toys around. I could play by myself or with others. Sometimes I played in the sand just for the fun of it, but other times I had a definite purpose such as building a castle or sand sculpture. As an adult, I find myself playing in different ways. Writing is now my sandbox. When I write I sift through ideas filling the page with words or dumping them out. I create things with words or just move my thoughts around. Sometimes I write alone, but I also write with others. Sometimes I write for fun, other times I write for a purpose. Writing for me is play.

———

HOW DID you play as a child? Did you do activities where time seemed to stand still or you did them just for the sheer pleasure of doing them? How do you play now?

Play is a spirit or energy, a way of being. Play is personal. When you play, you often lose all sense of time and you feel joyful. There isn't a right way to experience it. You can't force someone to play, you can only invite them. As we begin this journey, I invite you to play with me. Come jump in my sandbox and explore different ideas and ways of thinking. Sift through the ideas. Fill your mind with things you want to hold onto and dump out those you don't. Play by yourself or invite others to join you. Explore, experiment, and test out what works and what doesn't work for you. Play for fun or to create something. Let the stories inspire and motivate you. Imagine new possibilities for your students and you.

To play in the sandbox, you must lean in. You can't stand on the outside and play. You need to get in and get messy. Leaning in is messy and fun. Throughout this book I invite you to come alongside my story, to get in the sandbox and play along with me. In each chapter, I play with ideas, not because I have the answers, but because I don't. I play to explore, to experiment and to learn. I play to grow and to discover who I want to be for myself and others. I can play by myself, but I'd much rather play with you. Come play with me! **LEAN IN**.

PRACTICE - Lean In!

Have you ever leaned over a railing or stood on one of those glass platforms at the top of a skyscraper and leaned out? Leaning in can be exhilarating and fun, but it can also be terrifying. I remember the first time I visited Willis Tower in Chicago. There is an observatory at the top where you can step onto a glass platform and lean into the city. I could not step onto the platform. Even though I knew it was safe and it looked fun, I could not get my body to do what my mind was asking it to do. I could not lean in. I teetered on the edge, barely putting a foot forward, offering instead to take pictures as my children delighted in the experience. Despite the fact that I knew it was safe, I could not convince my brain and body to lean in. Our brains have an amazing instinct to keep us safe; sometimes too safe. This is difficult to override. Just ask someone who has a fear of spiders or flying. No matter how much they rationalize the fear, it can be debilitating and affect their ability to enjoy certain experiences or opportunities for growth.

———

GO AHEAD, move your body and lean in. What does it feel like? Notice how it takes some intentionality and control to lean. You need to push forward and yet hold yourself so you don't fall flat on your face. Leaning in emotionally or for a purpose has a similar feel. It's a push and a pull. You can play with the idea of leaning in, but really understanding it and implementing it takes practice. Practice is a way of doing something. Done repetitively, practice becomes permanent or a habit. So be careful. Some habits keep you from growing and becoming more of what you were meant to be. You want to practice behaviors and attitudes that push you to improve.

The tendency to pull back and stay safe occurs when we try to lean in and move forward emotionally or toward a purpose. Think about a time you decided to lean forward and try something new. What did your inner voice sound like? Did it encourage you? *That's a great idea, you can do it!* or did it try to sabotage you? *Who do you think you are? You can't do that? It will never work.*

I'll admit, I'm pretty risk adverse. I'd rather keep my feet on solid ground than lean into a glass box from the top of a skyscraper. I guard my emotions, too. I carefully think out my goals and ambitions, weighing them against my perceived abilities. These things keep me safe, but they don't allow me to grow. Fortunately, as this story played out part of me instinctually overrode this safety feature by leaning in. Maybe it was Mrs. G's cunning persuasion or perhaps my desire to serve others that pushed me past my secure boundaries. Whatever it was, the way forward depended on me leaning into this moment and this opportunity.

———

ONE WAY TO improve your ability to lean in is to practice it. Mel Robbins, a motivational speaker and author, shares an interesting technique you can practice in her book, *The 5 Second Rule*. The premise of the book is that if you try to lean into a new goal or change, your inner self will often try to sabotage your plans. Robbins has a five second solution to overriding this self-sabotaging instinct. Robbins explains, "if you have an impulse to act on a goal, you must physically move within 5 seconds, or your brain will kill the idea."[2]

One of the simplest ways to begin practicing this technique is with your morning alarm. I don't know about you, but I often hit the snooze hoping for a few extra minutes under the covers. But I would rather approach the day with enthusiasm. Wouldn't you? One thing that has worked for me is practicing the 5-second rule. When the alarm goes off, rather than hitting the alarm, I start the countdown 5...4...3...2...1! Before I finish counting, I jump out of bed and move. I brush my teeth and get a glass of water.

I will admit when I started this approach I had to set multiple alarms and place them in different rooms to force me to get out of bed and move. But it worked, and it can work for you too. Rather than snoozing into your day, lean in. In what ways might you practice this rule? How might you implement this rule in your classroom or family? How might you grow and change if you **LEAN IN**?

PURPOSE - Lean In!

BECAUSE OF 4 students, I leaned in. I didn't think I could do it. I didn't think I had the capacity. Having the courage to lean in allowed me to discover potential I never knew I had. Leaning in is more than just doing, it's being. It's daring to open your heart to possibility and opportunity.

Purpose is your reason for doing what you do. It's what engages, inspires and motivates us. Each of us has a purpose. We have a calling to discover our purpose and use it to serve those around us, including our students, families, and communities. What is your purpose in this moment? Who needs what you can give? In what ways might you lean in? You can do it. All it takes is 5 seconds. **LEAN IN**.

LEAN IN
step-by-step

4

Lean in to the sandbox. Get messy and have fun.
Play with ideas about goals you have or ways you might lean in.

PLAY

5 seconds is all it takes to lean toward a goal. Choose one from
above.Write an action step you are willing to take.

PRACTICE

How do you show up? Who needs what you have to give?
Name four students and tell how you might
lean in to be more for them. >AND
YOU!

PURPOSE

Create a Vision Board

LEAN IN AND think about the hopes and dreams you have for your child, students, players or yourself. Be open to possibilities and miracles. Start a vision board. Simply collect pictures, words and sketches that reflect or inspire the vision you have for yourself or your students. You can go all out and create it on a poster board or keep it simple and just use this page.

TWO

MIRACLES

BELIEVE IN MIRACLES

Do you believe in miracles? -Al Michaels[1]

FOUR BOYS STRUTTED in the hall, cafeteria, and playground as if they were the leaders of a parade. A nod here and fist pump there, clearly identified Rick and Larry as the leaders. Michael and Jerry sometimes served as sidekicks. Kids either gravitated toward the four boys or steered clear. These third grade boys were dynamite and only needed a spark to set off a spectacular grand finale.

I shuddered as a spark flew one morning while I monitored the cafeteria for breakfast. It began as Tom, a new kid, taunted the four boys. *Oohs* and *aahs* filled the air. I heard the sonic boom of footsteps as Tom ran out of the room with Rick and Larry close behind. On autopilot, I moved to head off the boys in the hallway. My heart pounded, but not due to my quick jog. I looked around for backup. As I realized I was the only adult around, my mouth jumped ahead of my brain and addressed the boys. "Hey guys, why don't you come over here and talk with me a minute?"

They stared, scanning me up and down. The only thing longer and colder than their gaze was my slow, deep breath. I tried to control my own rapid heartbeat and extinguish the potentially explosive situation. Rick nodded to Larry and plopped down in the student work area.

Tom stopped running and stood like a deer frozen by headlights, but his mouth kept going. Jabs and blame flew across the empty space. My attention moved back and forth as I played monkey in the middle. Finally, I leaned in, "Why don't you head back to class, Tom? I want to talk with Larry and Rick for a minute."

As he opened his mouth, ready to lob another insult, I shot him my best don't you dare look. You know the one parents and teachers perfect for just these kinds of moments. *Thank goodness,* I thought, as he snapped his mouth shut and turned around.

Words continued to fly from the boys, as I silently willed Tom to keep walking. I slowly exhaled as he walked into the classroom. Still the only adult around, I wanted to deescalate this situation as quickly as possible and get back to my own morning responsibilities. Looking past the squared shoulders and defiant eyes, I grasped for some way to connect with these two.

———

"SO, I LIKE YOUR FOOTBALL JERSEYS," I said noticing their youth team jerseys. "Do you play?" Blank stares and shrugged shoulders answered me. I forged ahead anyway. "What types of skills do you need to play football?"

"You know, run, throw, kick."

Disgust oozed in the distance between us. They couldn't figure out what I was doing. Why was I talking about football, rather than the hallway chase? *Fake!* They shouted with their silent expression and glaring eyes. I was fumbling, but I wasn't faking. Something electric pulled me in. Trying to harness the energy, I continued.

"Are you good at football?"

"Do you like to play?"

"What position do you play?"

"Oh, my son played that position. I was always afraid he was going to get hurt. Do you ever get hurt?" I drew our story away from the events in the cafeteria and began to lean into the boys. Piece by piece the wall between us crumbled. Their shoulders dropped and the curl in their lips opened to a smile.

"Yeah, I got hurt really bad once."

———

AS THEIR EYES SOFTENED, I pounced. "Look, you boys have a talent. I was watching you when I was in your class the other day and in the cafeteria today. I noticed you have an extraordinary skill. Want to know what I think?"

They looked at each other and back at me with the slightest glint of curiosity in their eyes. *Got 'em*, I thought, *hook, line, and sinker*. I leaned in to reel them in. "You are leaders. People watch you. Adults watch you. The other students watch you. I'm just wondering what type of leaders you want to be. It seems to me you have a whole lot of potential to really create some good in this school."

Sitting a little taller, they made eye contact. I leaned in a little farther, "Do you want to be seen as leaders?"

"Yeah," came the unexpected response.

I looked them square in the eye. I could almost feel them leaning in. "Well, it's too bad you're wasting all your talent trying hard to cause trouble. You are both amazing, but all your attention is focused on tearing people down instead of building them up. Leaders don't tear people down; they make everyone around them better. I would love to see what you could do if you were that kind of leader." And with that, I got up and walked away.

PLAY - Believe in Miracles

In cartoons when something like this happens, the characters stand with their mouths hanging open. I never turned around, so I'm not sure if I completely got that effect, but I do think the universe shifted that morning. Scientists would explain this shift using chaos theory and the butterfly effect.[2]

Chaos theory explains how small changes in initial conditions lead to much larger changes in results. According to this theory, the power initiated by a butterfly flapping its wings in New Mexico could eventually lead to a hurricane in China. This is called the butterfly effect.

There was certainly a butterfly effect to this moment, but I would explain it as a miracle. A miracle is the product of unwavering belief and extraordinary effort according to Hal Elrod. Hal is one of my favorite inspirational speakers and is the author of *The Miracle Equation*.[3] In this book he suggests we begin to create miracles when we set intentional goals to achieve results. This was the moment my miracle began.

———

WHEN I THINK OF MIRACLES, my mind always goes to the story of the 1980 U.S. Olympic Hockey team. Even if you're not a hockey fan, you can probably appreciate this incredible story. The American hockey team was composed of a bunch of college kids. They had little hope of defeating the mighty Soviets. But in the final seconds of the U.S. vs. Soviets game, the Americans took down the mighty Soviet team and won the opportunity to play Finland. In the final game against Finland, the U.S. team won the gold medal. The quote, "Do you believe in miracles?" was made famous by the sports announcer, Al Michaels, as he called this exciting moment.

While winning the gold medal was truly a miracle, it didn't happen by chance. It happened because Herb Brooks, the coach of this dream team, believed it, visualized it, and took the action and hard work necessary to make the dream a reality. Along the way, he built a team of believers from assistant coaches to the players themselves. He didn't quit, no matter what!

Coaches aren't the only miracle makers. Teachers and parents are miracle makers too. Creating miracles in students requires unwavering belief and extraordinary effort. You must believe in your students and children until they are able to believe in themselves. It's not easy. To build winning teams like Brooks, you need to apply Hal Elrod's formula: an unfailing belief in the potential outcome + extraordinary effort = a miracle. I BELIEVE IN MIRACLES. Do you?

PRACTICE - Believe in Miracles

Think back through your day. Did you have any small moments which might someday result in the butterfly effect? Can you see any places where you missed an opportunity to have a small moment and start a miracle?

I know sometimes it is challenging to be in the moment when there are so many demands on your time and energy. But whether you are a parent, teacher, coach or all three, any small moments you utilize to create a positive interaction and build relationship is a solid investment. My interaction with the boys lasted less than ten minutes, but it changed the trajectory of our relationship forever.

———

ONE SIMPLE THING to practice is how you interact and react with students. I sometimes find myself focusing my expectations on desired results rather than on the child. I might point out something the student needs to work on, whether it be a skill, behavior, or attitude. While I usually do this out of love and concern, to the child it may come across as disappointment or that they are not good enough. Brené Brown shares a wonderful blog about how an interview she heard with Toni Morrison changed her parenting paradigm. In the interview, Toni asked, "when a child walks into a room, does your face light up?"[4] She explained how you might think you are displaying your love and affection when you check to make sure your children have their pants buckled or hair combed, but what the child sees is a critical face. She suggests your face needs to convey the love that is in your heart.

Your face can light up for your children or those in your care. All you need to do is lean in and look for something positive in them, even if they don't see it in themselves. You can use your face to show children you believe in them, and that you believe they are miracles.

————

SMALL MOMENTS often occur unexpectedly and in unlikely places such as the cafeteria, hallway, playground, or dinner table. But you don't have to wait for them to happen, you can practice building small moments with something as simple as smiling and interacting during meal time.

This is often an overlooked opportunity for parents, teachers, and coaches. I know I've hurriedly put down food at the table or groaned at the idea of another hockey team dinner, rather than investing in these as moments to connect with my children or players. But my work in the cafeteria gave me a front row view of the butterfly effect.

At first, I didn't fully appreciate how important this time is for some children. My own children are fortunate to get breakfast at home. I make it my goal is to start our day with a positive outlook. The more time I spent in the cafeteria with students, the more I realized this is not true for many kids who show up in the breakfast line in the morning. By the start of their school day, many students are already tired, hungry, and knocked down.

The breakfast scenario itself can be daunting for students and the staff assigned to monitor it. It's loud and messy. Someone always spills their milk on the carpeted part of the floor or somehow sprays the cereal across the room when they try to pull back the sealed plastic lid. Kindergartners struggle to balance a tray in front and an oversized backpack behind them. Kids need help; they want to talk, and everyone needs to be done eating and the tables clean by the time the bell rings. Some kids are happy, and others walk in with a chip on their shoulder bigger than Mount Everest.

I saw this time as an opportunity to be a miracle starter. I would smile as I wiped up spills and tables. When students ran up to me to tell me they remembered me teaching them in their classroom, I would talk with them about what they learned or how they are being a good thinker. I would smile at as many students as I could, saying, "have a good day" and "work hard."

———

IF SHARING a meal is not a typical practice for you, it may feel uncomfortable at first. While it can be awkward for teachers and coaches, it can be equally challenging for parents. It helps to have a topic or something to talk about. You can talk about a favorite piece of music, a book or something the student is reading, or even use conversation cards. You can change the tone by making it more of an event. At home this might mean eating in the dining room or putting a tablecloth on the table. Coaches can host pre- or post-game celebrations. In the classroom it may mean sitting down with students in the cafeteria or inviting them to a more formal lunch by sending a formal invitation or bringing in some fancy dishes.

I once greeted all my small student groups with a tea party using my good china. We only had water, but the change in environment and expectation was impactful. Students sat up straight and tried to engage in conversation like they were the king or queen.

No matter how you choose to set up the experience, the true power of the butterfly effect is in the interaction and in the relationship that is built through it. Let your face shine and reflect your belief in miracles. In what ways might you use a small moment to build a relationship with a student? How might you grow and change if you BELIEVE IN MIRACLES?

PURPOSE - Believe in Miracles

BECAUSE OF 4 students, I believe in miracles. I believe miracles are built over time with unwavering faith and consistent action. They start with small moments which grow to have a larger impact. An unexpected moment changed the trajectory of my relationship with four students. Imagine what moments are waiting for you.

Do you believe in miracles? You can start a miracle with a moment and a smile. Let your face light up the next time a child walks into the room. Sit and enjoy a meal together. Create the space for a moment to share a smile or initiate a conversation. Look around. Who needs a miracle? Where might you create a small miracle? You can do it. All it takes is for you to **BELIEVE IN MIRACLES**.

BELIEVE IN MIRACLES
step-by-step

Miracles happen when you believe they can. Play with ideas you have for using small moments to create miracles.

PLAY

Time spent in relationship creates miracles.
Identify a time & place to connect with someone to make a miracle.

PRACTICE

Your belief in a student creates miracles.
Name four students and describe how you might
create a miracle for them. >AND
                                    YOU!

PURPOSE

Create a Habits Tracker

Miracles = unfailing belief + extraordinary effort

HABITS ARE essential for supporting beliefs and sustaining extraordinary effort. What are some habits you currently use to support your beliefs and efforts? What are some habits you would like to develop or encourage in yourself or your students. Use this space to record and track your habits.

Habits	Sunday	Monday	Tuesday	Wednesday	Thursday	Friday	Saturday

THREE

4

HABITS

THIRST FOR LEARNING

All kids do learn, but not on the same day and not in the same way. -
Arthur Costa[1]

"BOYS, why don't you try walking along with me? As leaders, you can demonstrate being respectful in the hallway," I emphasized in my best teacher voice as the boys practically ran down the hall to my classroom. The carefully laid out games tumbled off the table as they entered the room like bulls in a china shop. "So, here's how this game goes," I explained as I tried to pick up the game and they grabbed for the pieces and cards.

"I'm going first," Larry announced.

"What makes you think you get to go first," retorted Michael. "You always think 'cause you play football you are the best. You ain't always gotta go first."

"I'm not playing," interjected James with his hood pulled down way over his eyes. "It's not fair."

"Here, let's roll the dice and the highest number will go first," I said feeling much like a referee in a wrestling match. The air in my miracle balloon was quickly deflating. This was not at all what I had signed up for. Games like this are supposed to be fun. My own kids hadn't acted like this since they were about four years old. *Haven't these boys ever played a game?* I thought to myself. My statement to "remember you are leaders" was greeted with grunts and eye rolls. Time slowly ticked by as I did my duty, feeling more and more help-less and inept. It's only for a few times, I thought silently, feeling slightly discouraged, but still hopeful.

———

AS I WENT to get the boys for our next session the following Monday, my mind raced. I hadn't prepared as well as I had hoped. A busy afternoon of administrative duties had taken most of my time and energy. I struggled to think of how I could let them display their leadership skills and get in lots of physical movement. *What can I have them do with their hands?* I wondered, half pleading with the universe for an answer. As I corralled them down the hall, I decided to pull out the Keva[2] blocks. One of the teachers on my team raved about all the activities we could do with them, but I hadn't had time to look up lesson plan ideas. I felt like I was grasping at straws.

"Let's try something different today. I have this giant bag of blocks and I'm not exactly sure what we could do with them. There are cards showing how to build things, but I thought it might be fun to see how high of a tower you can build." I introduced the activity, being careful to make sure the goal was for the boys to build their best tower, not to compete against each other. Teamwork and competition were goals for another day. Today, I just wanted them to play.

Being unfamiliar with the blocks myself, I grabbed a pile and started building. The boys just watched for a few minutes, uncharacteristi-cally silent and still. Blocks are fun. I always enjoyed playing with blocks as a kid and with my own kids. I smiled as I began building and looked up at the boys.

"Come on," I said. "It's fun. Try something. You really can't do anything wrong." I honestly was just trying to make it through our time together, but something else was stirring. They started building…and talking…and I started listening. I started writing what they were saying on the board.

"This is a fun challenge."

"I'm going to finish."

"Help me make it."

"This is hard."

"Let's do this!"

"Oh, cool!"

"This is really fun!"

"I'm trying."

"I'm not losing on this."

"I have a new idea."

"I like Mondays now."

As we wrapped up our time, I pointed out to the boys how their conversation had shifted. We talked about how they were practicing habits as I pointed to the posters around the room. *Habits of Mind* (Costa & Kallick, 2000)[3] was one of the main focuses of my small student groups. Posters of the habits hung around my room. I often used posters, activities and discussions to help students learn these sixteen habits and foster intelligent thinking. Together, we identified some of their talk as persisting, flexibility, and responding with wonderment and awe. My own mind was no longer racing like it was at the beginning of the session. I had found a straw to grasp. I was on a high. We connected and there was hope.

PLAY - Thirst for Learning

For these boys, connecting with a teacher in a positive way was a new experience. My experience with school had been much different. Over the years, I built strong relationships with many of my teachers. Some of those relationships are still standing today. My kindergarten teacher, Mrs. Wright, came to my college graduation and helped me get my first job. My first grade teacher, Mrs. Czupeck, handed me my diploma as I graduated high school and attended my wedding. I am still in contact with both of them.

One of the best examples of a strong relationship I built with a teacher came just after I got my first teaching job. I walked into my empty classroom and found a small package on my desk. I opened it to discover a small wooden board with random objects such as a jack, eraser, staple, a tiny purple plastic monster glued on it, and a label with the words *Miss Murphy's Thing-a-ma-jig*. Tears welled in my eyes. I had made this board for my second-grade teacher. She had saved it all those years. Upon hearing I got my first teaching job, she gifted it back to me. It sits proudly on my desk. It's a reminder to me of how much a teacher can do to help a student believe in themself.

Miss Murphy was one of my favorite teachers. She had all kinds of crazy sayings, like "thing-a-ma-jig" It inspired me as a young student to make one for her. She was not an easy teacher, but I knew she loved me. She brought out the best in me. When I was frustrated by noise she would whisper, "noise is a torture to all intelligent people." When I was quiet and had trouble making friends, she told my parents I was a "silent leader." When I struggled with math and numbers, she noticed I was a good writer and showcased my writing ability and let me do special projects. It's a special kind of teacher who gets to know the best in her students, loves them enough to stay in touch with them, and even saves the crazy things students make for them.

I don't really remember what I learned in second grade, but I do remember how I felt. Even now when I think of Miss Murphy's classroom, I remember feeling happy and safe. This day with the boys had the exact same feeling, but this time I was the one creating the experience. I was the teacher with the crazy sayings who was embracing my students for who they were. When I did, it was like watching a butterfly emerge from a cocoon or a flower blooming. It was magical, watching them open up and allowing me to teach them.

———

SOMETHING SHIFTED IN THAT MOMENT. These boys didn't have the love of school I had as a child. Many of their interactions with teachers and adults were filled with reprimands and critique. They didn't know how to let down their guard and play or be creative. They had high emotions and high energy, often causing confrontations with other students and adults. But on this day, everything aligned, and for the first time they learned being intelligent isn't just something you are born with or measured by a test score, it is the way you act when you don't know the answers and it feels good. You could see the excitement in their eyes and the energy in their voice. They were loving the learning experience.

Whether you are working with a child in the classroom, at your kitchen table or on the field, much of what you are teaching them goes far beyond academics and skills. You are instilling the foundations and habits to encourage them to be lifelong learners. You inspire a **THIRST FOR LEARNING**.

PRACTICE - Thirst for Learning

Have you heard the saying, "You can lead a horse to water, but you can't make him drink?" I have a horse and I can tell you; it's true. I can lead him right to the water and he will not take a drink. We often use this saying to make excuses for why we are not able to get students to do something we think is good for them. When I have this challenge with my horse, I give him salt. While I can't make him drink, I can make him thirsty. We can do this with students too.

When we give students salty lessons, activities or learning experiences it makes them thirsty for learning.

Salt enhances the flavor of foods. It can also make you thirsty. Good teachers engage students and enrich lessons to make students thirsty for learning. One way they do this is by teaching scholarly habits. Costa and Kallick call these scholarly habits, *Habits of Mind*.[4] In their work, they identify a set of 16 *Habits of Mind*. These habits represent some of the intelligent behaviors displayed by successful people. They are skills such as metacognition, listening with understanding and empathy, and taking responsible risks.

Scholarly habits enhance learning by providing students with the ability to access and engage in the experience or environment. These positive learning opportunities are like a salt lick for a horse; they make them thirsty for more.

———

INTELLIGENCE IS MORE than just knowing answers. It's how you behave and react when confronted with challenging problems. Arthur Costa and Bena Kallick (2000) refer to this as *Habits of Mind*. These are the same habits I noticed the boys using in our lesson. In their book, *Learning and Leading with Habits of Mind*, Costa and Kallick explain the purpose of teaching these habits stating,

"when we teach for the *Habits of Mind*, we are interested also in how students behave when they don't know an answer. We are interested in enhancing the ways students produce knowledge rather than how they merely reproduce it. We want students to learn how to develop a critical stance with their work: inquiring, editing, thinking flexibly, and learning from another person's perspective."[5]

I was fortunate to learn about the *Habits of Mind* in a workshop directly with Arthur Costa himself. His love of learning and students is infectious. Reading his words in the book is intellectually stimulating by itself, but hearing him speak and his passion for creating learners and scholars is incredibly moving. Throughout his career he has continuously looked for ways to engage kids with the habits. He encourages teachers to use and adapt his work. He has compiled book lists and movie lists to illustrate the habits. He has also partnered with the Association for Supervision and Curriculum Development (ASCD) and WonderGroveLearn[6] to produce animated videos illustrating the habits. The animated videos and lessons are ready-made for teachers to use as a tool to bring these habits into their classrooms.

TEACHERS AND SCHOOLS can also directly teach the habits through activities, literature, and discussions. There are many resources teachers have shared on the internet as well as in the *Teacher Resource Library* curated by James Anderson.[7] While these lessons are great for introducing students to the habits and the mindset, what really matters is continuous use and reinforcement. Consistently drawing attention to practicing and using the habits is necessary to shift them from something students learn about to something students do automatically.

Teaching students *Habits of Mind* is about creating an atmosphere and mindset where these habits can flourish. One of the simplest ways to begin teaching them is to simply hang up the *Habits of Mind* posters in a classroom or home. James Anderson of *Succeeding with Habits of Mind*[8] has compiled a wide range of resources and supports for helping teachers bring *Habits of Mind* to life in their classroom. Among these, he provides a free set of posters[9] to print and utilize in the classroom. Colored versions are also available for purchase in the store. When these posters are in a visible location, they can be utilized in the moment to focus a student on a particular habit or to foster reflection on the learning experience. After a lesson, a teacher can simply ask students which of the habits they found themselves using during that time.

———

WHEN I BEGAN to listen to the boys' conversations in my lesson, I recognized them using the habits. I hadn't taught them the habits yet, but it was a perfect opportunity to help them recognize what it felt like to learn and to use *Habits of Mind*. In the moment, I was able to capture their words and show them how their thinking aligned with the habits. Teaching isn't always about planning the perfect lesson. Sometimes it's about teaching when the perfect opportunity presents itself. When students are thirsty for learning is the perfect time to teach scholarly habits. In what ways might you teach scholarly habits? How might you inspire a THIRST FOR LEARNING?

PURPOSE - Thirst for Learning

BECAUSE OF 4 students I make students thirsty for learning by teaching scholarly habits. Long after the details and facts are forgotten, the love of learning and the habits instilled will linger. Sometimes these moments are planned, but often they are seized, as real life challenges present opportunities to develop essential skills.

Thinking skills and *Habits of Mind* are tools students need to solve the complex issues in our world today. Teachers, parents and coaches can't possibly teach students everything they need to know, but they can provide the salt for them to be inspired lifelong learners. What are the skills or habits your student needs to succeed? How will you inspire a child? What salt will you use? Teach scholarly habits and inspire a THIRST FOR LEARNING.

THIRST FOR LEARNING
step-by-step

Teachers bring out the best in students by noticing and inspiring them. Play with ideas you have for engaging and inspiring students.

PLAY

Teachers provide the salt that makes students thirsty for learning. Identify scholarly habits you might use as salt to inspire a thirst for learning.

PRACTICE

Inspire a student, teach them habits and they will be thirsty for more. Name four students and a scholarly habit you could use to inspire them. >AND YOU!

PURPOSE

Create Space for Moments

ONE OF THE most important habits to work on is being present in the moment. Life is often so hurried and busy that it is easy to get caught up in what didn't get done or what you still need to do. Reflect on some ways you can be more mindful of your daily actions and more present in the moment.

FOUR

MINUTES

BE IN THE MOMENT

The time is always right to do what is right. -Martin Luther King, Jr. [1]

HAVE you ever stopped to think how things can change direction in a matter of minutes? A storm can blow away a town; an accident can alter a family; an act of hatred can destroy a country; and a single decision can change the course of a life.

A hero's journey is never without challenges and with each step forward I seemed to take two steps back. The next time we met was a whole different story. I finally felt like maybe we were getting somewhere, but as soon as I picked up the boys I knew something was different. There was a substitute teacher in the boys class which meant the four boys were spread out in different classrooms. We had already learned these four could not be in the room together without Mrs. G. We had created a plan to move them to different classrooms when there was a substitute teacher.

They were in rare form. Angry jibes were the only things I heard as I maneuvered them down the hallway, hoping to make it to my classroom without an incident. I reconsidered my plans for the group session based on their moods. Another teacher had borrowed my blocks and I was planning to introduce them to circuits. Now, I was concerned about placing a $200 box of Little Bits[2] circuitry in their hands given their current emotional state.

"I wanna play a game. You said we could play a game," James said grabbing a game off the shelf.

"No, I wanted to build a robot. She said we were going to build robots," Michael retorted.

"Look, why don't we see what you can do with these puzzles today?" I said, hoping I didn't sound as hopeless as I felt. I was starting to think maybe this would be one of the last times with this group. I had done my duty. I'd let them come for a few activities. We talked about how they could be better thinkers. After all, I really didn't have time to take any more students. I was just working with them for a few times to help with their attitudes. We had one good class, but it was becoming clear this was probably more of what I could expect from these boys. Somehow the puzzles went well. I'm not sure why. It often seemed the boys did better when their hands were engaged in an activity. Michael, James, and Larry worked on one together and Rick went off to a table by himself. I was relieved when our time was up.

———

NOW FOR THE *walk back down the hallway*, I mused. I kept them moving somewhat quietly and together. But as we turned the corner, my heart sank and then leapt to my throat. Rick took off running the other direction. *What was he doing?* I thought. *What happened? How do I get him and still walk the other boys down the hallway without an escort? Should I call for back-up?* Without more than a few seconds hesitation, I sent the three boys down the hall alone, as they continued to protest and grumble. I quickly turned and headed the direction Rick had run, not knowing what to expect.

Every bone in my body shouted with fear and anxiety. Rick was tough. Really tough. It wasn't his size, it was his eyes. Years of trauma caused him to build a protective wall around himself using his eyes and body language. Although I saw glimmers of a spark in his eyes, most of the time he stared through me with an intense beady-eyed look. He was only a third grader, but I was slightly afraid of him.

As I turned the corner expecting the worst, I saw him curled up and shaking in a little cubby by the bathrooms. I couldn't tell if he was angry or crying. Not knowing how to approach him, I simply decided to use a technique I use with my daughter. Rick's hiding in a small space reminded me of her fear reaction. When she was upset, I would find her curled up under a desk or in the farthest corner of her closet. This had been happening more frequently as she felt like school was overwhelming and all her teachers hated her. In those moments, I would simply sit and be with her. I knew I couldn't get close to Rick, but I was pretty sure I could let him know it was ok.

AS I SAT on the floor near him, I said, "Look, I can tell something is bothering you and you probably don't want me here right now. It seems like you could use some time to cool down. How about joining me in my room while I clean up the puzzles? You can eat lunch, relax, and calm down with me, but I won't bother you. It's hard with a substitute teacher and I know you need a few minutes before going back to class."

"Fine."

We walked down the hall in silence. He grabbed his coat for recess. He had been assigned to another classroom for the day, so I updated the teacher about the incident and our plan for lunch. She nodded knowingly. Rick and I walked down the hall. Even after the walk and time to cool down, I was surprised to see the smoke coming out of his ears. He wasn't just upset, he was angry. I had no idea what had happened to set him off or how to relate to him. I was just hoping I could calm him down enough so he wouldn't cause trouble at recess or back in the classroom.

We walked to the lunchroom and picked up his lunch. His usual strut was replaced with a slow, sullen saunter. We brought his lunch to a table in my classroom, pushing aside the puzzles left strewn about. He started moving the pieces of the puzzle around. I sat quietly. I concentrated hard on breathing calmly. In and out. In and out.

———

HIS BREATHING SLOWED and then he talked. "I've never done that before," he mumbled under his breath.

"What?" I asked, having no idea what was going on or where this was going.

"Walked away from a fight," he whispered, continuing to move the pieces of the puzzle into place.

Woah! I didn't even realize there was a fight in the making. What had I missed as we walked out of the classroom? What was going on here? *Don't talk too much,* I thought to myself. *Listen.*

"How did that feel?" I managed to ask.

He shrugged.

"You know, you remind me of someone. Have you ever heard of Martin Luther King, Jr."?

"Sure."

"He was great at speaking and persuading others, just like you are. He also never used violence. He believed we could make more of an impact by protesting peacefully."

"He never fought."

"I don't think so. Let's see if we can watch some of his *I Have a Dream* speech."

We watched a few minutes of the speech, and I watched the calm return to Rick. He kept working on the puzzle and continued to calm down.

"Do you think I can go to recess now?"

"You tell me. Are you ready?"

"Yep," he replied and jumped up, heading outside.

I watched him enter the playground a much different boy than the one who had run down the hallway earlier. I found the teacher from his assigned classroom and updated her on the situation.

"It's amazing he trusted you with that," she commented. "You've really made a huge difference. He's such an amazing kid, if we can just help him."

I walked back to my office with mixed emotions, both slightly overwhelmed with remaining work and optimistic of the changes I was seeing in him and myself. I just hoped I had calmed him down enough. I wrote a note for him to take home. I wanted him to know I was proud of his courage to avoid a fight and his work to calm himself down.

———

IF I HAD any doubts about whether I was making a difference, I just needed to wait one more day. As I was heading out of the school for a meeting, I saw Rick down the hall. Rather than displaying his usual indifference, he ran into me with a barrel hug. It caught me completely off guard. Here was the toughest third grade boy I knew, hugging me in the middle of the hallway. The four minutes I had taken to meet Rick where he was in the cubby and the time I spent with him over lunch made a difference well beyond the moment. Because of those four minutes, nothing was ever the same.

PLAY - Be in the Moment

For some reason, even as this story was unfolding I was keenly aware of what was happening. Although I had somehow missed the event causing Rick's anger, I quickly tuned in to what he needed from me rather than what I needed from him. The moment of connection between us was so strong I can still feel the exact moment when everything shifted. Richard Davidson (2019)[3], a neuroscientist who studies the mind, body, and spirit connection explains this in an interview with Krista Tippet. According to Davidson, the same mechanisms that allow adversity to get under the skin also enable awakening.

When teachers provide students with tools to calm their bodies and emotions, their bodies are able to function better. Davidson further suggests teachers actually change students' brains, functionally and structurally. This statement is not as radical as it seems, because in fact we are changing each others' brains all the time. This occurs in a parent-child relationship and in any kind of sustained interpersonal relationship.

The social-emotional aspects of learning and education are strong. One of the key aspects of cultivating this type of interaction and creating stories which move us in a more positive direction is mindfulness. Mindfulness is a state of being present and focused on what is happening in the moment. It is often developed through practices such as meditation. Mindfulness teaches you to develop an awareness of the present moment without judgement.

———

WHEN THIS IMPROMPTU lunch with Rick occurred, I had been following a daily meditation practice for about a year. As a result of this practice, I was able to control my own emotions and breathing. This allowed me to exude calm. I gave Rick mindful space, but close physical proximity to me. It allowed him to mimic my breathing and my calm. It also pulled him out of his state of anger and anxiety.

This story could have had many different endings, but I believe my mindfulness practice helped pull our stories together and have a positive outcome.

I first learned about mindfulness in a breakout session at a conference. The presenter talked about how she developed her own mindfulness practice to help decrease postpartum depression and then began using it with her AP students to help them handle the anxiety related to exams. She shared the results she gained for herself and her students. I knew I wanted a similar outcome for myself and my students. I was ready to bring mindfulness into my class right away.

I did what most teachers do after a conference, I immediately started looking for resources and curriculum to bring into my classroom. At the time, mindfulness in the classroom was a fairly new topic. I didn't start right away, but instead started to look for more research and examples of how to do it. I came across the book, *The Way of Mindful Education* by Daniel Rechtschaffen[4]. A main premise of the book is to personally practice mindfulness before attempting to teach it. One quote early in the book stood out to me. "We often leap forward, wanting to help our kids relax, forgetting to notice how anxious and in need of relaxation we are. A teacher would never try to lead a math lesson if she didn't know the multiplication tables" (Rechtschaffen, p. 42).

I know I'm a leaper. I see a great idea, expand on it with a Google or Pinterest search, and try it out right away. I felt like the quote was speaking directly to me. Deep down, I knew I was bringing much of my own stress and anxiety to my relationships with my family and to my students. I was intrigued. I wanted to know more about mindfulness. It turns out mindfulness has a long history.

———

MINDFULNESS PRACTICES ARE DEEPLY ROOTED in various religious practices especially those of the Eastern traditions such as Hinduism and Buddhism However, the current Western movement was popularized by Jon Kabat-Zin, founder of the Center for Mindfulness at the University of Massachusetts.[5] In 1979, Kabat-Zin began introducing and researching the effects of mindfulness to relieve chronic pain and stress disorders. Since Kabat-Zin's ground-breaking work, psychology and education have realized the potential of this practice to improve health, emotional well-being and learning.

Current research[6] shows mindfulness positively impacts stress reduction, working memory, focus, emotional reactivity, cognitive flexibility and relationship satisfaction. Individual health can benefit, too, with research[7] showing pain reduction, decreased blood pressure, and improvement in physical conditions such as psoriasis and fibromyalgia.

———

IN EDUCATION, stress reduction has become an increasingly hot topic as neuroscience continues to reveal how damaging stress is to our learning ability and overall health. As Rechtshaffen (2014) states, "when our nervous systems are on high alert, or when we are flushed with self-critical thoughts, then our working memories function poorly, our creative juices do not flow, and our collaborative capacities are stymied." [8]

While stress is a major issue for our students, it is also a challenge for teachers, parents and coaches. The Mindful Schools[9] website has many resources to help teachers and families learn more about mindfulness and begin a daily practice. Richard Davidson's work with the Kindness Curriculum through the Center for Healthy Minds[10] also provides useful tools and research about how mindfulness and kindness can be cultivated in classrooms. Explore mindfulness for yourself and **BE IN THE MOMENT**.

PRACTICE - Be in the Moment

Small moments can result in big changes. In 2004, news anchor Dan Harris had an on-air panic attack on ABC's *Good Morning*

America. It was Dan's changing moment. For him, that moment led him to discovering meditation to manage his anxieties and overcome addiction. He eventually shared his story in a book, *Ten Percent Happier: How I Tamed the Voice in my Head, Reduced Stress Without Losing My Edge, and Found Self-Help That Actually Works – A True Story*.[11] Since then Harris has also launched a podcast and app[12] to help others learn to meditate.

Through meditation, Dan discovered his time spent in mindfulness practice had results far exceeding the expenditure. Dan proclaims the many benefits of meditation including lowering blood pressure, rewiring the brain, regulating focus and increasing self-awareness. He claims meditation helped him gain an edge rather than being edgy.

While we might not all suffer from a public panic attack, we have plenty of moments in our lives where we just keep going through the motions. We often move through our life on autopilot rather than on purpose or with intention. Mindfulness is about creating the time, space, and practice to choose how you show up for yourself and others. Personal experience and research illustrate how these few minutes create an impact far exceeding the investment.

Getting started with mindfulness is easy. But remember, the best way for you to bring mindfulness to others is to bring it to yourself first before you start pushing strategies on your class, children, or athletes. When you are mindful it changes your reactions and actions. This is one of those things you cannot teach until you learn it yourself. You might be able to teach the mechanics of it, but unless you learn it and make it part of your daily practice, you will not change. When you begin practicing mindfulness, your students will change because of how it changes you. After all, what you practice, you become.

———

THERE ARE many different ways to practice mindfulness from doing simple breathing exercises to blowing bubbles. When I first started exploring, I was overwhelmed with all of the options. I found short guided meditations worked best for me. In my classroom I often use simple breathing exercises. I have students breathe out for a count of 4 and breathe in for a count of four. Exercises like that only take a few seconds but can have powerful results in helping to calm bodies and focus attention.

Ready to try it yourself? Find a quiet spot, a timer and about four minutes. For me the most challenging part was finding four minutes in my day in a quiet spot where I wouldn't be interrupted. Throughout the first week of my mindfulness practice, my family continuously interrupted me. When they finally gave me time alone, mindfulness became nap time and I fell asleep. It took more than a year before I developed a consistent practice. When I finally did, I began to experience noticeable changes. I lost my temper less; I was less frustrated; I was less emotional. I was able to relax more, pay attention more, even breathe more. I was more calm, more connected and found more time to practice.

Where can you sit for four minutes? Sitting really is key here. As you begin this practice, laying down almost always turns into a nap. Although you probably need a nap, try scheduling that in separately. Sit quietly, put your hands on your lap and your feet solidly on the floor. A cross-legged position on the floor is also an option if comfortable for you. Sit tall with your back straight. Limit physical distractions as much as possible with your seated position.

Set a timer. If you choose to use a phone as your timer, make sure all your notifications are off. Remember, this is your quiet time. The world can wait four minutes. Close your eyes. Now breathe. Breathe in for a count of four, hold the breath for a count of four and then release the breath for a count of four. IN...2...3...4.... HOLD... 2...3...4...OUT...2...3...4. That's it.

At first it can feel like the longest four minutes of your life. As you breathe, your mind may wander in many directions. Just notice the wandering as if observing an image, and then come back to focus on your breath. Each time your mind moves to something else, embrace it as an opportunity to practice returning to your breathing.

––––––

SIMPLE, right? Simple, but not always easy. When you are ready for the next step, check out the many resources for developing a mindfulness practice. I personally enjoy using the app, *Calm*.[13] I enjoy the quality and variety of resources to incorporate mindfulness practice into different aspects of daily life. You can try for free but extended use requires a paid subscription. Teachers can obtain free subscriptions as part of the *Calm Schools Initiative*[14] dedicated to reaching 100,000 classrooms. Try it for yourself. **BE IN THE MOMENT!**

PURPOSE - Be in the Moment

BECAUSE OF 4 minutes with one student, everything changed. Months of practicing mindfulness a few minutes at a time prepared me to be present in the moment. Rather than simply reacting, I was able to respond with calm and empathy. My practice provided me the skills to create a space for Rick to change his response and behavior patterns.

Quiet your mind and nurture your focus. The skills you develop will extend beyond your practice and flow into all aspects of your life. The moments spent in mindfulness practice cultivate your ability to be present for yourself and others. In what ways might you practice mindfulness? How might this practice impact you and the children in your care? All it takes is 4 minutes - or perhaps 1 or maybe even 10; whatever will make it a daily habit for you. **BE IN THE MOMENT.**

BE IN THE MOMENT
step-by-step

PLAY

A change in a student can occur in a moment.
Play with ideas you have for being in the moment.

PRACTICE

Mindfulness practice reduces stress and improves your
reactions to it. Identify ways you might practice mindfulness
or increase your awareness of moments.

PURPOSE

Moments spent in mindfulness practice impact your life and
others. Name four students. Meditate on how you
might be in the moment for them. >AND
YOU!

FIVE

SCHOLARS

WHAT'S YOUR WORD?

If you want to change your life, begin by changing your words. Start speaking the words of your dreams, of who you want to become, not the words of fear and failure. -Robert Kiyosaki[1]

FOUR TEACHERS SAT across the table from me. No one smiled. I sat silently as each one told me how my daughter didn't want any help, so they were no longer trying to help her. The conversation in my head flowed like a waterfall. *What do you mean you don't help her because she doesn't want it? We are the adults. We are teachers. We don't have the luxury of saying we won't help students because they don't want it. We believe in them until they believe in themselves. What if I had given up on my four boys when they didn't want to learn?* I didn't speak any of those words out loud, but simply nodded while trying to hide my tears.

"Thanks for coming, Mrs. Peterson. We have another 504 meeting now, so please sign this paper and we'll send you a copy."

As I sat in my car, the tears began to flow. My heart felt as if it were torn in half. Why couldn't anyone else see what I saw? Why couldn't they see her amazing spirit and creativity? Couldn't they see the scowl facing them was fear? Didn't they know how hard it was to copy down notes, memorize facts, be called on in front of others and never get a chance to explore ideas, get her hands on things, watch before doing? They didn't know her stories leave me begging for a sequel, her photography pulls me into images I've never noticed, and she has ideas far beyond anything I've ever imagined.

I wanted to scream. We were making plans to move in the middle of her eighth-grade year. She was struggling not just academically but emotionally. She needed empathy, not indifference. I needed empathy, not a paper to sign and a quick kick out the door.

Why do we continue to tell students what they can't do without giving any credit to what they can do? Even when it doesn't match the curriculum. Where is the room for seeing talents outside the traditional classroom expectations or lesson plan? Why don't we see our students first and the curriculum second?

———

I THOUGHT about the four boys. We had been working together for a few weeks now and I was noticing a difference. As I got to know the four boys better and build our relationship, my focus began to shift from teaching to learning. I began to focus on their strengths and continued to look for opportunities to help them learn and be more of who they could be. One day, I started calling them scholars. It started when Michael commented he wasn't smart.

"What do you mean?" I questioned.

"I mean I'm dumb. I can't read."

"Of course, you CAN read!"

"No, I can't read good."

I responded quickly and without thinking. "You can't read good, YET," I added. "Don't forget the YET." I'm a big fan of the word yet. It's a powerful word for cancelling out the negative effects of "can't." I almost automatically add in the word *yet* when others tell me they can't do something. My heart ached for Michael.

This same sense of failure paralyzed me and my own kids in our personal struggles to learn to read. I remember crying over books, not being able to make sense of the words as my mom patiently practiced with me and found phonics games to make it fun. With my own kids, I would pull them onto my lap and read to them, making sure time with the written word was pleasant. This was sometimes a challenge as their own reading difficulties often resulted in tears.

Unlike with my own children, I couldn't scoop him up in my arms and hug him reassuringly. I would need another way to show him how special he was and show him he could get better at reading. How was it possible a nine-year-old boy could feel dumb? There was so much learning left to do. I wanted to grab an eraser and wipe his slate clean of every negative feeling he had about reading, school and himself.

I looked at the boys and asked, "Is that how you all feel?"

Shrugs and downcast eyes were the only response I received.

"Look at me," I whispered and slowly looked each one of them in the eye. I could see the spirit behind the shame. I could see there was something there. I don't know how to describe it other than a spark, or a glimmer. I see it as the moldable potential of each person. It's the innate sense of desire students have to be good enough. Sometimes it's hidden. Or perhaps sometimes teachers, parents and coaches don't have the capacity to see it. I don't know what it is, but I know when I see it. I also know I choose to be careful with it. Words can fan it into a flame or extinguish it all together.

"Smart only gets you so far. After that you need to work hard and be persistent. You don't want to be smart; you want to be a scholar."

"What's a scholar?" they responded with a hint of curiosity and a whole lot of attitude.

"A scholar is someone who loves to learn and works hard. Remember when we worked with blocks, and I recorded all the different things you were saying? You were being scholars. You were loving to learn, and you were working hard."

———

SCHOLARS. I had never called a student that before. It had come up in a reading with the leadership team a few days earlier. We were reading the book, *Switch*[2], about how to change when change is hard. In one chapter, a second-grade teacher used a similar definition of a scholar with her students and inspired them to be scholars. As a result, a class with low achievement scores rose above grade level by the end of the year. It seemed to be the right thing to say to the boys at the time. Never in my wildest imagination did I realize what this word would do.

Mrs. G chose to use the word also. "Let's show the other classes how a scholar would act in the hallway," she would say during this often-difficult transition time. The class would hold themselves up a little straighter and could be heard having conversations about something they had learned rather than budging to be first in line. Mrs. G's line became a procession of students engaging as scholars together.

"I'm a scholar, too!" exclaimed kids to me as they saw me in the hallway. At first I thought perhaps it was just a word they were copying. But then they would explain to me that it means they work hard and love to learn. I'd often use these moments as an opportunity to connect further and ask, "What do you like to learn about?" Their eyes would get a sparkle or glimmer and they would tell me passionately about something they were learning. Sometimes it was school-related. Often, it was some other topic.

"I like to learn about bugs. I got this book from the library, and it has like 1 million different bugs in it. There's this one bug...."

"I'm writing a story. I have 20 pages right now. It's going to be a whole book."

"I'm learning about hockey. I'm trying to figure out a great play so we can get more goals."

I began using the word scholar in all my groups and in my interactions with students whenever it fit. Even at the school breakfast, I began sitting at tables talking to kids about how they could be a scholar. "Scholar" quickly became more than a word; it became an identity.

PLAY - What's Your Word?

In teaching, some things are planned, and others are inspired. When I was studying teaching in college, one of my professors read from a poem book every day. One morning, I found myself being bothered by the poem he read by Albert Cullum. One of the lines stuck with me. It read, "The geranium on the windowsill just died, but, teacher, you went right on."[3] Instantly, my brain flashed through previous teachers who seemed to miss events like the geranium; instead, they continued to teach their lessons. It reminded me of how I felt they were missing important things going on around us.

Although it's been more than 25 years since I have heard that line, it still haunts me. Throughout my teaching career I caught myself living this line more often than I would like to admit. This time, when the geranium died with the boys declaring they were dumb and couldn't read, I stopped. I could have continued with my lesson and not dug any deeper. But I didn't. I intentionally chose to understand how the boys were seeing themselves, and, from that, I was able to discover an opening for creating a new self-image. The word *scholar* held power because I believed and they believed, not just in the word, but in the image of themselves it created.

———

TEACHERS UNDERSTAND the important relationship between words and academic achievement. Sometimes, vocabulary is the initial reason students struggle to understand content and concepts.

Almost any teaching guide includes key vocabulary. Sometimes words are also part of the academic content or discipline. Knowing and successfully using discipline-specific words is what Sandra Kaplan refers to as "Think Like a Disciplinarian."[4]

This concept can help students develop the language and skills of the discipline teachers are teaching. For example, rather than just learning math, students learn to think and solve problems like a mathematician. Rather than simply coloring a map, students might learn how a cartographer constructs maps and how to use similar tools and vocabulary to construct a map. Rather than just writing for an assignment, students are encouraged to be a writer and write for a purpose or audience.

Shifting the focus to include the discipline as well as the content can help provide the big picture for students and encourage them to think like the vocation and to use the words specific to the content areas. Even tiny shifts could open the doors for students to connect with the vocabulary and content. Coaches can also use this by connecting the skills they are instructing with how it is used in actual games and by professional athletes. They can emphasize sport specific language. Parents have many opportunities to point out how various skills around the home and in learning are applied by professionals in the real world. They also have many opportunities to engage their children in conversation and extend their vocabularies.

Sometimes the power of words extends far beyond academics. The poet and educator, Albert Cullum, was a powerful advocate for infusing the classroom with words, creativity, and play. In the documentary, *A Touch of Greatness*[5], his teaching is captured illustrating his belief that teachers have "the priceless opportunity of giving each child the gift of believing in him or herself." Words can open doors to understanding literature, history and all the disciplines and they can also open doors to our hearts, allowing us to believe in our own potential. Give students the gift of words to build them up as scholars so they can work hard and love learning. **WHAT'S YOUR WORD?**

PRACTICE - What's Your Word?

Words are powerful. One of the most tangible examples of this is Chris Pan's *MyIntent Project*.[6] In 2013, Pan received an intention bracelet for his birthday. He chose the word *impact* for the bracelet because he wanted to remind himself to make a difference. Pan started making these bracelets for friends and soon discovered the power of the conversation and words.

What started out as a small personal project grew into a full business. Pan continues to emphasize the importance of the conversation and connection in this project. The word bracelet is a powerful tool for connecting people with words that inspire them. "What is your word?" is the slogan of this project.

I believe my mindfulness practice and current reading enabled the word scholar to surface for me. It aligned with many of the habits and ways of thinking I was trying to grow in my students. It resonated with me. The word wasn't powerful, however my belief in it was. It was just waiting for the right opportunity for it to become more than just a word. I simply had to capture the moment when it presented itself.

———

TRY this exercise to help you find your word and be open for the moment to use it and make it stick. Think about words which might have the power to connect your child, students or athletes with their potential in a positive way. I like *scholar* because it works across all disciplines and supports the ideas of hard work and developing thinking skills. Words like leader, athlete, helper, learner, responsible, generous, imaginative, confident, or motivated might work better for your purposes.

One word of caution here from my experience as a gifted specialist. I often work with students who have been given the word 'smart'. This word can be particularly harmful in supporting what Carol Dweck[7] defines as a fixed mindset. Students with a fixed mindset attribute their success to things outside of themselves and beyond their control such as intelligence or 'smarts'. When confronted with a challenge or obstacle, rather than working to develop the skills or knowledge needed to solve the problem, they quit because they don't believe they have enough of this trait. Words encouraging effort are better for fostering a growth mindset, allowing students to see their ability to learn and solve problems.

Whatever word you chose, don't just throw it out at a student. You must believe it and believe in the power it holds for the student to move forward in a positive direction.

———

PETER REYNOLDS[8] has some great books for creating opportunities for students to look at how they might be limiting their potential with the words and attitudes they hold. One of my favorites is *The Dot*[9]. In *The Dot*, the main character, Vashti, decides she can't draw. When her teacher turns her angry attempt to make this point into a work of art, she realizes perhaps she can draw after all.

Every time I read this book with students; they catch on to the theme immediately. The students make dot artwork to illustrate their unique creativity and potential. This can be a great way to get to know students at the beginning of the year. Consider celebrating International Dot Day[10] at the beginning of September where you can connect and celebrate with other schools and students.

You may also want to look at this lesson by Julie Ballew, *The Power of Words: Teaching with the Dot*[11]. Julie's word is *encourage* and she wants to encourage her students to outgrow themselves and hear her voice cheering them on. She also wants them to "understand that they have an opportunity and an obligation to lift up a classmate, every single day." After using the Reynolds book to prompt a discussion about the power of words she has her students create their own dot art with encouraging words.

Because of a word, four scholars were created. One word allowed them to grow into a better version of themselves. What words are you putting into the world? Do your words create and inspire? Because of four scholars I believe in the power of words. You can too. Choose your word. Inspire greatness. **WHAT'S YOUR WORD?**

PURPOSE - What's Your Word?

BECAUSE OF 4 students, scholar became a schoolwide identity. One word allowed students to grow into a better version of themselves. Words matter. They can crush spirits, be a tool for inspiring change or develop academic discipline.

Choose your words carefully. Choose words to inspire and build up, to open possibilities rather than limit your options. Discover which words motivate you to reach your goals, bring you joy, or move you to greatness. In what ways might you use words to encourage yourself? How can your words encourage others? One word may be all it takes for you to become more of who you are destined to be. **WHAT'S YOUR WORD?**

WHAT'S YOUR WORD?
step-by-step

Words are academic tools and powerful motivators.
Play with ideas you have for using academic and motivational words.

PLAY

The words we choose can impact how we perceive ourselves
and the world. Identify words you might use to encourage
yourself or students.

PRACTICE

Words matter.
Name four students. What's your word for them. >AND YOU!

PURPOSE

SIX

LETTERS

IT'S PLAYTIME!

Play is serious learning. -Mr. Rogers[1]

IF I HAD any illusion my lunch date with Rick was a one and done, I was strongly mistaken. As soon as I got to the classroom the next time to pick up the boys, I was barraged with questions and pleas.

"How come Rick got to have lunch with you?"

"When do we get to eat lunch with you?"

"Can I eat lunch with you again, please...please, I'll help you clean up."

I realized the 30 minutes of extra time I had squeezed in for this group would now include lunch. I'll do lunch with them, I thought, hesitantly. While I knew eating lunch with students was well worth the investment, I struggled with competing demands for my time. I was often scheduled to attend meetings or travel to other buildings for duties related to my role as gifted coordinator. I was torn.

"Ok, I can't today because I have another meeting, but let's see how things go today and I'll look at adding it next time. I really want to try something today, though. I want you to start being scholars. I'm going to get the Little Bits²out, but we must think like scientists, and we must be careful. I can't have you guys fighting and throwing things around. Ok?"

I didn't really know why I thought this would work. We'd had a few good moments together and they really seemed to be interested in acting like scholars, but everything else I tried resulted in angry insults or disinterest. I thought about how my own kids and I would play and make things together.

Give my kids a page of homework and you would think the world was coming to an end, but a box of scraps yielded hours of endless fun, creativity and problem solving. Once, on a snow day, they turned our entire kitchen and family room into a marble maze and spent hours testing their contraptions. I was secretly hoping this session would help the four boys let their guard down and realize how much fun it can be to learn, just like when we were building in our first session.

The Little Bits kits contained circuits and wires. Students could connect the various pieces to a battery, using switches and sliders to turn on a light, create a sound, or move a motor. Each box came with lesson plan ideas, but most of them focused on the teacher showing the students what to do. I wanted to let go and let them play, but I also didn't want to lose pieces or have them broken. I wanted them to trust me, but the truth was I really didn't trust them. How many times had I told other teachers to let go and believe in their students? *Believe in them, let them play*, I chided myself.

———

I OPENED the lid of the Little Bits kit and set it on the table in front of them. The boys immediately leaned in and started grabbing and touching pieces.

"How do these work?"

"What do we do?"

I took a deep breath and reaffirmed my resolve to believe in their ability to explore something new. "I guess you are just going to have to be scholars and try some things and learn. I really don't know how they work."

The boys stared at me for a few minutes, probably trying to assess what kind of teacher doesn't know what she is teaching. I wasn't sure what I would do if they didn't start exploring on their own because I truly didn't know what most of the parts did or what exactly we were going to do with them. I couldn't blame them for being wary of my motives. I hoped they sensed my honest uncertainty. More than likely, they were just genuinely interested in the new toys. They shrugged their shoulders and turned to building.

At first, as they pulled out circuits and wires with questioning looks, they would show me and ask, "what does this do?"

Each time I responded with a shrug and said, "I don't know. I have this book and we can look it up," as I flipped through the book. Disgusted with having to read to get an answer, they left me to the reading and started testing the circuits themselves. This approach was vastly different from the one my other groups took the day before.

Those groups carefully read through the directions and then stared at the circuits as if they might bite. After a whole class period, they hadn't even figured out how to hook up a circuit to the battery. Today, these four boys grabbed the battery first, plugged something in, and marveled at what they were able to create.

Everyone had a sense of discovery, with animated gestures and loud voices. As the boys continued to explore, a playground of lights and buzzers emerged as parts were continuously connected and reconnected in new ways. I relaxed into what was happening and let go of my fear of losing pieces.

A strange sense of awareness overcame me. I watched the symphony of play before me and smiled at the music wafting to my ears. Time seemed to freeze. Laughs erupted as things worked or didn't work. Walls came down. This time the fuse that was lit led to a very different kind of dynamite.

"Look at this!"

"Oh, it's a fan. Cool!"

"Listen to this, guys," shouted Rick as a buzzer continuously sounded from loud to soft with lights dimming and glowing in concert.

"Does anyone know what this does?" I asked, jumping in and making my own circuit.

"Yeah, use this little screwdriver thing and you can change the color of the light," Michael explained.

Anyone who walked past my room would probably think it was chaos, but I knew it was beautiful. For the first time, we all let our guards down and worked together. As I walked the boys back to class that day, I didn't have to remind them that they were scholars. They walked through the hall with their heads held high, their eyes lit up, and their voices animated as they continued to discuss what they wanted to do with the circuits.

———

I DIDN'T KNOW where I was going to find the time or how I was going to make it work. I wasn't following the regular protocol for identifying these four boys as part of a group, but I knew what I needed to do. I knew the right thing to do was to make this group permanent. My lunch conversation with Mrs. G sealed the deal.

"I think I need to invite the boys to the EXPLORE group and make it official. I know I didn't identify them in the screening, but they are exactly the types of students we are hoping to serve. There is some-thing there. What if I go ahead and send home invite letters today?"

"I think it's the right thing to do. They are really something special."

They sure are, I thought, heading to my meeting. This time they had me hook, line, and sinker. My mind was going a million miles an hour thinking about all the things we could do with the Little Bits and how I could continue to help them see themselves as scholars.

———

"I GOT THE LETTER," was the first thing from Jerry's mouth when I picked him up the next time. "My mom is so proud of me. She wants me to be a scholar, too."

I smiled. "Well, let's get started then, scholars," I said, willing the magic to continue.

It's PLAY time!

Mr. Rogers would have been proud of this lesson. This moment was playful. I finally let my guard down and trusted the boys, allowing them to trust me. I used my training as a gifted specialist to encourage creativity and problem solving. Because Little Bits were new to me, it was a chance for me to be in the moment with my students and let them see me as a learner and explorer also. I was able to model my learning strategy of reading and looking for ideas while also respecting their mode of engaging in active play.

In the *Sweet Spot*, Christine Carter[3] describes this moment of connectivity as a positive emotion amplifier. She explains when we smile and interact in a positive way, our brains and brain activity begin to connect and mirror each other. Our shared emotion, such as joy, leads to a shared physiology. As our heart rate and breathing synchronizes, so does our body language. We literally open up and create a signal allowing others to let down their guard and open up too. It is essentially a signal to play.

While many consider play to be just fun, Dr. Stuart Brown[4], a pioneering researcher on play, believes it is essential. In studying prisoners, Brown's research revealed deprivation of play in child-hood as a common thread in their histories. Studies with animals reveals similar findings. In a research study on rats, the rats were placed into two groups. The first group was deprived of play, the second allowed to develop and play normally. When these two groups were exposed to a cat scented collar, the group whose play had been deprived refused to come out of their cave and eventually died. The playful group continued to venture out and test regardless of the real danger. Further studies on play reveal nothing lights up the brain like play and we all recognize and respond to signals of play.

In his TED talk, Dr. Stuart Brown, further explains, "the opposite of play is not work, but depression."[5] As Dr. Shimi Kang, author of *The Self-Motivated Kid*[6] stresses, play is a critical ingredient to our social, emotional, and physical development. She argues the unstructured, free opportunity to explore different ways to do some-thing leads to several benefits. According to Kang, play allows us to:

- Make mistakes and learn to take failure in stride
- Discover new things
- Have fun
- Develop team skills
- Improve our ability to innovate and create
- Regulate our emotions and deal with new challenges

Play is one of the earliest and most natural teachers. Parents take advantage of this all the time with their young infants. I remember my daughter as a toddler in her highchair. I believed one day she would be able to hold a cup to drink a glass of milk or water without spilling it all over herself and the floor. But as she transi-tioned from a bottle to cup, I didn't just hand her a cup of milk and hope for the best. I gave her multiple opportunities to prepare and experience holding her own bottle and bringing it to her mouth.

In the bathtub or sandbox, I gave her a cup and she picked up water or sand and dumped it out. I put a lid on the cup so she could be successful at taking a drink without spilling. All the time, she was learning and having fun developing this new skill. Did I teach her how to hold a cup? Did I provide direct instruction as to how to hold a cup and bring it to her mouth? No. I let her do the work of children. I let her play.

———

I HAD a similar opportunity to experience playful learning when my friend's cat had a litter of kittens. They would jump, pounce, and roll around with each other. They could chase a feather on a stick for hours. What were they doing? They were jumping, leaping, reaching, catching. They were learning the skills they needed to interact with their environment, catch their food and leap out of danger. Did the mother sit and meow directions to them? It didn't appear that way. She sometimes pulled them back into the shelter when they wandered too far for their skills, but over time she allowed them to roam until they were able to go out on their own. She watched and protected, but she let them play.

I brought two of these kittens home when they were old enough and they now are confident, masterful barn cats. They know how to survive and fend for themselves. A few years later we got a kitten from a shelter. It had no siblings to play with and no mother to provide a safe environment for play. This kitten was fearful and shy. It was never able to transition to be a barn cat because it had not developed any instincts or skills to survive on its own.

In the learning process, play is more than just an activity. It is a mindset and an interaction. Play isn't optional. It's an essential ingredient for teaching and learning. **It's PLAYTIME!**

PRACTICE - It's Playtime!

I can still remember the morning my dad called my brother and I into the kitchen with unusual excitement. We ran in, expecting the most exciting news we had ever heard. After holding the suspense for a moment, he finally said, "today we are going to play Tom Sawyer," and led us out to the garage.

"What is that?"

"How do we play?"

"Where are we going?" We continued to barrage him with questions while he handed each of us a paint brush and carried the bucket of paint to the backyard fence.

"Now we paint the fence," he said and got to work. We grabbed our paint brushes and began painting with gusto. We had half of the fence painted before we realized playing Tom Sawyer was really hard work.

———

I HAVE ALWAYS KEPT this experience in mind as I taught. When I taught third grade, one of the most difficult parts of my year was teaching writing. Our state assessment included a writing component in which students were given 40 minutes to construct an expository, descriptive, or narrative essay. As pressure to improve test scores increased, I found myself resorting to more direct and rote instruction. Writing became a chore rather than play. One day, I decided it was time for a different approach.

When it came time for writing, I rubbed my hands together, smiled at the students mysteriously and told them "Today we are going to use our writing skills to write the best story ever, but you need to follow the rules." The first rule was to not do anything until I told them.

The students eyed me suspiciously as I handed a sheet of paper to each of them. A few started to write their names and I quickly reminded them of the first rule to NOT put their names on the paper. Since this was usually my first direction, it caught their attention. When everyone had a sheet of paper, I asked them to close their eyes and visualize a story, real or imaginary, and play it in their head like a movie. After a few minutes, I told them to stop and write down the first sentence of their story. A few groans ensued but I pressed on.

"Now," I said with great seriousness and drama, "fold your story into a paper airplane." We had recently made paper airplanes for a science unit, and I had confiscated several paper airplanes for disrupting our learning. So of course, they were surprised and hesitant.

"Come on, make paper airplanes," I urged. When everyone had a plane, I reminded them to follow directions.

"When I count to three, throw your airplane across the room. Be careful and don't throw it directly at someone. Then when I say, GO, pick up the airplane closest to you." I held my breath and hoped this was not the moment the principal would decide to do an observation.

"Ready? One, Two, Three." Airplanes flew across the room.

"Now, go!" Everyone grabbed an airplane. Then I told the students to open the airplane, read the first line and continue writing the story. We continued adding details, a climax and finally endings to our stories. In the end, we read them aloud and laughed. Over the next few weeks, the stories provided useful examples and mini lessons for what techniques worked and didn't work in the narratives. Everyone was interested because we weren't just giving feedback on one student's work, we were focusing on everyone's work. Narrative writing had never been so much fun for my class, and my state scores were the highest they had ever been. These scores seemed to be a direct result of allowing the third-grade students to incorporate a playful approach to our otherwise tedious writing lessons.

———

ACCORDING to Brené Brown in *The Gifts of Imperfect Parenting*,[7] play is an activity in which we experience joy and lose our sense of time.

It is personal. When we play, we experience a chemical surge of dopamine in our prefrontal cortex which encourages us to cement the learning and to pursue this type of activity again. Dr. Stuart Brown's[8] research identifies several different types of play. Think about how you participate in each of these types of play and how you might encourage more of it.

- **Physical play** – Imagine a goat leaping into the air or a child jumping into a pile of leaves. This type of play involves the whole body and is often done for no reason other than the sheer joy of it.
- **Object play** – The manipulation of objects like forming a snowball or tinkering with blocks or mechanical objects. The ability to connect the hand with the mind has been shown to increase problem solving ability.
- **Social play** – The ability to connect with others and create meaningful bonds is often seen in our ability to play with each other. Therefore, play is a critical part of the early childhood learning experience.
- **Rough and tumble play** – Although researched mostly in animals, this kind of play is a strong teaching tool. All species participate in some type of rough and tumble play.
- **Spectator and ritual play** – As humans we experience this type of play most often through our sports and team competitions by experiencing the play and cheering on the players.
- **Imaginative play** – The ability of a child to engage in fantasy and build imaginary worlds is an amazing play activity to witness. This form of play is often used by great artists as they first imagine their ideas before bringing them into reality.

———

BUILDING play into your classroom or home is not as much about creating time or opportunities for play as much as it is a mindset.

Bringing more play into your life or classroom can begin with a few simple questions. These appreciative inquiry questions modified from the work of Michelle McQuaid[9] encourage you to think about times when you are feeling playful and to focus on how to replicate those opportunities.

- *When you (or your student) are engaged, energized, and enjoying life what's happening?* This question pushes you to think about what is happening or what you are doing when you are experiencing the benefits of play, engagement, energy, and joy.
- *If you could get more of what you've just described consistently, what might be possible?* This question pushes you to identify how you might intentionally plan for playful activities. If different members of a family or class have different ideas about what is fun, how might you combine these into a playful activity for all?
- *How can you move from where you are to where you want to be?* Do you have a vision for where you would like to be? This question encourages you to create a path from where you are now to where you want to be.
- *If there was one action you could take, where would you be willing to start?* Changing behavior requires a first step. What step are you willing to take to create more of what you want in your life, family, sports field, or classroom?

Questions like these and creating opportunities to connect and build relationships with students can open the doors to more playful learning. You can plan for these experiences, but play can be spontaneous and unplanned. Be open for those opportunities too.

You can apply a sense of play to almost any chore or lesson. You can ask a student or class to help redesign activities, so they are more playful. Most coaches use a variety of games to reinforce skills. Focus on play as a mindset, not an event. Use playful analogies in your vocabulary. Be playful. Provide play signals to your students by engaging in activities with them, sharing your passion and knowledge for the content. Don't just send your students onto the playground, run along-side them. Don't just push your children on the swing, swing along with them. **IT'S PLAYTIME!**

PURPOSE - It's Playtime!

BECAUSE OF 4 students I was reminded of the importance of play and my role in creating those opportunities and sharing play signals. Playing allowed the four boys to experience the world around them and the joy of learning. One session of play broke down years of anxiety and hostility toward teachers and created an opportunity for learning to occur.

Although a natural activity, sometimes we hesitate to play. We see it as a waste of time or a frivolous activity. But play is rarely a wasted activity. It is a mindset, not an event. It provides many opportunities to learn and creates a spirit open to learning. Are you stuck? Have you lost the joy of learning? In what ways can you bring more play into your own life? How might you play with your child, students, or athletes? If you want students to learn, **IT'S PLAYTIME!**

IT'S PLAYTIME!
step-by-step

Play is an essential ingredient in learning.
Play with ideas you have for adding more play to your life, interactions,
or teaching.

PLAY

Appreciative inquiry is a useful tool for recognizing opportunities
for play. Using the appreciative inquiry questions, identify a
playful action step to take today.

PRACTICE

Play is a mindset, not an event. Name four students and tell
how you might encourage more play for them. →AND YOU!

PURPOSE

CREATE A PLAYLIST

CREATE a playful mindset by thinking back to some of your earliest play memories. How did you play? What worlds did you create to play in? How did you imagine you would change the world? Use this space to reflect on your many, varied and unusual ideas. Need more help? Laura Haver, a play advocate, has created an awesome playlist exercise to help you create your own list of playful activities. Look for her resources at https://linktr.ee/Laurahaver.

SEVEN

IDEAS

CHANGE THE WORLD

What do you do with an idea....You change the world. -Kobi Yamada[1]

"GET your lunches because we are all eating together today," I said as I met the boys at the door, barely getting the words out before they were already running back to their cubbies to grab their lunches.

Now, we all looked forward to Monday mornings. In a few short weeks of meeting, the stall tactics and avoidance behaviors they used for almost everything related to school were replaced with enthusiasm. Rather than having to wait for them, they were now waiting for me at the door and admonishing me if I was even a second late. It took seconds instead of minutes for them to grab their lunch and rather than leading them down the hall, I had to quicken my pace to keep up. As we reached the classroom, I shared my plans.

"Let's really work on being scholars today. We are going to make notebooks for you to keep track of your ideas. If you want, you can also put on the lab coats and goggles." I really didn't think they would be interested in wearing the lab coats or goggles. The way these boys strutted and showed off their colors and labels, there was no way they were going to be caught dead in a lab coat.

"Cool!"

"I want the green googles."

"Here, Michael you be red."

"Yeah, you can be green if you want. I'll take the blue ones."

———

I STOOD AMAZED, barely able to grasp the scene playing out before me. If you had asked me a few weeks ago where would these boys be in ten years, I might have just shook my head sadly. Today, if you lined them up next to their past selves, you wouldn't even recognize them and the only line I wanted to see them in was one that led to graduation. I wanted them to break every statistic and grow up to be the men I knew they had the potential to be.

I could picture them walking across the line to get their diploma and being there to hand them their diploma just as my first-grade teacher, Mrs. Czupeck, handed me mine. I still remember how amazing it was to see her as I reached for my diploma. Although it had been a long time since first grade, she was a teacher I admired and stayed in touch with over the years. She was a school board member and happily took the opportunity to hand me my diploma with a hug.

That's what I wanted for these four boys. I wanted to continue to be a part of what they were becoming. I saw a future for these boys as they continued to dress themselves up in both attire and actions as scholars.

———

IDEAS

THE SCOWLS in their eyes once filled with distrust and anger were replaced with smiles and enthusiasm as they reached for the box of Little Bits. Even before they got started the negotiating began.

"Can we stay in for recess and work with the Little Bits longer?"

"You're ok with missing recess?" I hadn't anticipated this extra time and while I was encouraged by their enthusiasm, I also worried about my nagging to do list and how they would manage with the extra time.

"Yeah," was the collective answer.

"Ok, let's see if we can really build something today." I wanted to be present and playful with them, making the intentional choice to tackle my own list later.

As the boys finished adorning their scholarly attire and putting together their notebooks, they also started pulling out pieces of the Little Bits. "Let's build a car."

"Yeah, let's do that!"

Over the next hour, the magic I previously experienced settled in again. The boys built and rebuilt. They put things together and took them apart. They had long since given up on asking me what to do with pieces and began turning my ignorance into a bit of a joke. "Why is it turning like this? How do I get it to go straight?"

"Don't ask her, Michael. She doesn't know anything about this. She'll just look in that book and tell you to figure it out. Look, see this button? When you move it, it goes like this."

"I need a screwdriver."

"What kind?" I asked.

"A small Philips," Rick responded without skipping a beat.

"How do you know the different kind of screwdrivers?" I asked, thinking about my own time working with my dad in the workshop.

On Saturday mornings as my dad worked around in the yard or garage, I learned to use a hammer to pound nails into a board. Old skates became skateboards and leftover boards a playhouse. Alongside my dad, I learned not only the name and use of his tools but how to care for them and use them properly. I learned rules you couldn't find in books, like "never force anything" and "always put things back where they belong."

Rick shrugged as he continued snapping in pieces and flipping switches. "I help my dad sometimes. It's just something I know." I nodded understanding completely.

———

WHEN IT WAS time for lunch, I could barely get their attention because they were so absorbed in building. "Do you want to take the lab coats and goggles off when we go down to the lunchroom?" I asked, sure they would be more concerned about upholding their image than their scholarly identity.

"No way! We want everyone to see we are scholars."

As the boys stood in a line in the hallway for a photo I demanded, Rick jumped in front and waved me off. "You have to turn the collar up on these coats to make them look cool," explained Rick as he went around making sure everyone looked cool.

"Yeah, we're gangsters," exclaimed Larry.

"No, you are not gangsters," I said suppressing a laugh. I put on my most serious face and looked them in the eyes. "You are scholars now."

"Oh yeah, right. Scholars." The boys strutted into the lunchroom. I couldn't help thinking about the poignancy of Larry's statement. Usually, they strutted into the lunchroom like gangsters. Today something was different. As much as tough third graders could, they were strutting like scholars.

We brought their lunches back to my classroom but they barely touched them. I did my best to mother the boys and remind them to eat, but they couldn't contain their excitement about building more with the Little Bits. "Why don't we build two cars? Look, there's enough stuff here to build two." They exclaimed opening another Little Bits kit.

My heartbeat quickened again, partly from enthusiasm and partly from the realization I would now have to sort out tiny pieces from two mixed up kits. I vowed to remain playful and allowed their enthusiasm to surpass my worry.

"Yeah, let's work in teams and race."

"Michael, you work with me and Jerry and Larry can work together," directed Rick.

"You always work with Larry," questioned Michael.

"Yeah, let's try it this way today. You and Jerry sometimes have trouble," responded Rick with authority.

Rick was like a well-oiled machine. He seemed to instinctively know how to put things together to make them work and embraced the leadership role that accompanied his new-found confidence. The other boys, normally reluctant to let anyone take the alpha role, seemed to bow to his orders. They didn't just work along-side each other, but together. Each time a piece popped off or they couldn't figure something out, I started to tense up thinking the magic would end, but it didn't.

"It's not working."

"YET...don't forget the YET," smiled Larry with a slight nod my way. It was funny hearing my words come out of his mouth in much the same way I sometimes now hear my own mother's words coming out of mine.

"Yeah, we can do this. Just keep trying." The pieces continued to pop off and they built and rebuilt. Suddenly the already electrified air sparked, "We got it! Look at this!" exclaimed Rick as the car began rolling down the hall.

"Quick, let's get this other one working so we can race."

"It keeps going in circles. How did you fix that?"

"Try this button here, remember I had to use the screwdriver."

"YES!"

———

THE BOYS LINED up at one end of the hallway and I grabbed my iPad to record. I signaled the start of the race as if it were the Indy 500. "Ready, Set, Go!"

They were off. The boys jumped in and out of the race path, cheering on their cars. While the cars poked along at a turtle's pace, the enthusiasm and energy in the hall made it feel more like the final stretch of a major race. Somehow, I had enough time to begin worrying about what would happen when one of the teams inevitably lost.

Despite my mindfulness and all of the positive momentum we had gained, I was often brought back to the reality that they were still working on developing social and emotional skills. The boys and I were still works in progress in terms of mindfulness, forming positive relationships, and developing scholarly habits. They loved the winning part of competition, not so much the losing. My worry was wasted.

———

"WE WON!" shouted Rick.

Larry immediately slapped him on the back in a congratulatory way, "You sure did! We all did. We made a race."

PLAY - Change the World

Rarely are we aware of the small moments that make a difference. Often looking back we can identify those markers in life which turned out to be crossroads where things could have gone many ways. Reflecting back it is easy to see how these turning points carved out our paths. But these life changing moments often slip through our days unnoticed. I knew the significance of this moment. Not only did I snap a million pictures in my mind, I grabbed my iPad and recorded as much of it as I could. Several of my shots only captured images of the floor as I got so wrapped up and excited in what was happening.

So many things converged to make this moment. I could never have planned it and honestly, we never quite captured it again. The energy moved beyond our little moment, as the boys presented their success to the principal who happened to be available. They were familiar with being sent to the principal, but never for something good. Watching the pride and excitement in their eyes as they demonstrated what they accomplished was amazing.

These four boys who struggled to read and write words were masterful engineers. They believed they could; they collaborated, persisted and celebrated. In the weeks to follow, all my other groups experimented with the Little Bits. Although many were able to create something they had envisioned, the total effect created in this moment, by these four boys, was never replicated.

———

THIS WAS one of the most successful lessons I have ever taught. But how do I prove it? What measures can be used to validate this assumption? There are many ways to measure educational results, from assessments of ability and achievement to rubrics and grading checklists. Much of the current rhetoric in education is focused on measurement as the key to educational reform. We focus on setting goals and standards so we can measure the outcomes and cost.

The entire "No Child Left Behind" educational policy was focused on setting these measurable outcomes and then evaluating whether students and schools met the standards. There is an entire assessment industry built around creating tests and measures of everything from intelligence to reading ability. Nothing in this mass of evaluation research fits.

No assessment or rubric can accurately objectify the success of the four boys that afternoon, racing their cars down the school hallway. The same hallway where they once intimidated others. The same hallway where Rick made a new choice to avoid a fight. That day, in that hallway they supported one another in an amazing display of character development. Perhaps the best description of what happened comes from Dr. Suess' famous line about how the Grinch's heart "grew three sizes that day."[2] I know my heart grew and opened to the boys in a way I never experienced before. I also know their hearts opened as they experienced a joy and success in learning they had never known. I don't know how to measure it any other way, nor am I sure I should.

The assessment rhetoric has tried to convince us that success can only be determined by their carefully crafted measures of reading and mathematics. But are these the measures that count? At what cost? There's a quote often attributed to Einstein, "Everybody is a genius. But if you judge a fish by its ability to climb a tree, it will live its whole life believing that it is stupid."[3] Although Einstein probably didn't say it, it's a pretty good statement.

The four boys in this story believed they were stupid and gangsters until they were put into a different pool. Given water rather that a tree, these fish were able to show they could swim. Yes, their skills in reading and math are important and need to be developed, but the cost of continuing to focus on their deficits rather than strengths is too high.

———

IN ANY OTHER SETTING, these four boys were lacking executive function skills. They were easily distracted and would give up. They had trouble following directions and would display tantrums over minor issues. In their classroom, they displayed challenges in remembering what they read or following a sequence of steps. If the boys did not possess these skills, why then were they able to display them in this setting?

The secret may be found in the motto of MIT, "Mens et Manus,"[4] which translated means mind and hand. This motto is not only a guiding vision at MIT, but a way of life. As a result of this culture, MIT has defined itself as one of the leading schools of innovation in the world.

Schools across the country are beginning to realize the effects of our singular focus on reading and math to the detriment of other subjects such as science and social studies but also in fitness, the arts and in the increase in issues related to a loss of executive function skills. As a result, not only have reading and math skills failed to improve, but the steady decline in these other skills has created severe challenges in behavior, apathy and poor school performance.

The solution to such challenges is as complex as the challenges themselves, but perhaps a key to unleashing the potential of some of our nation's most challenging students is to connect their mind and hands. Let them turn their ideas into real things and give them hands-on opportunities to **CHANGE THE WORLD**.

PRACTICE - Change the World

Mind and hand connections can transform teaching and learning. I experienced this firsthand in my work as a gifted specialist. In meeting with a group of teachers who worked with the gifted and talented students in our school, our conversation turned to how all our students could benefit from the types of activities we did as enrichment. We discussed and brainstormed ways we could enable kids to have a "mind and hand" experience, so all teachers could see firsthand the benefits of these activities.

In our brainstorming, one of the teachers shared a video about a little boy who created an arcade[5] out of cardboard. At that moment, we knew we had our idea and decided to put together a school mini golf course. Just like any other district, we had standards to meet and test scores to improve, but we managed to convince the administration and the entire staff to devote just one day to building a course.

As our district was learning more about design thinking, it was the perfect opportunity to use it to create this experience for our students. We planned lessons and introductory activities and presentations to fight every reluctant teacher. Our gym teacher agreed to make golf his last unit of the year and to let the kids 'play' the course for the final week of school. We secured donations of cardboard from some amazing local sponsors and parents.

Students, teachers and staff built a golf course. Our district media team captured the day[6] and a local newspaper[7] promoted our story. While you can see and hear the excitement of the students in the video and story, they can't capture the conversations I had with teachers. Almost every teacher talked to me about a student in their classroom who wasn't doing well in reading or math or was challenged with behavior, who excelled as a mini-golf course designer.

Teachers who worried about how they would have enough for students to do for a day or half day were commenting on how they wished we could do this all week. In subsequent years, rather than this being a single day event, teachers incorporated design thinking into their various units so students could have an opportunity to explore with their mind and hands throughout the year.

———

CONNECTING the mind and hand is not a new idea. John Dewey,[8] the pioneer of education, proposed all learning is experiential in nature and relied on students having both opportunities to engage in real experiences using their hands and to use their mind to reflect on those experiences. Several movements in education have also captured a similar spirit. The Maker Movement began gaining traction in 2006, when Dale Dougherty created the first Maker Faire as part of a media campaign connected with his factory, O'Reilly Media and its launching of *Make* magazine. Dougherty, in designing the fair, used digital tools and knowledge to bring together people who made things. Not only was the fair wildly successful but it started what is now known as the Maker Movement[9]. Many educators have jumped on this bandwagon[10] realizing the opportunity of its ideals to shift education from consumption to creation.

In a similar spirit, A.J. Julliani began toying in his classroom with an idea he had learned from Google in which their employees were encouraged to use part of their time to explore their own interest or projects. He created a Genius Hour[11] in which students were encouraged to spend one hour a week pursuing a topic of their choice. The concept has sparked an enthusiastic following of teachers as well as increased interest in a related idea called design thinking. As A.J. Julliani worked in his classroom, he began to use design thinking as a strategy for moving students through the learning process. In continued work and partnership with John Spencer, their collaboration produced a guidebook, *Launch,*[12] for teachers to use this process. They also developed a way for teachers to join this movement called the Global Day of Design.[13]On this day, teachers involve students in making and creating things using the design thinking process.

———

IN MY OWN work with gifted students, I developed an approach to inquiry learning called IDEAS.[14] IDEAS is an acronym which guides students through the following steps of the inquiry process.

- Imagine possibilities and identify a topic.
- Develop a learning plan and questions.
- Explore answers and connections.

- Announce to an authentic audience.
- Self-reflect and evaluate

I further developed it when working with a group of homeschool students in a co-op. I discovered it is something that can be taught to all levels of academic ability and multiple grade levels. It is also a process I teach to teachers at the university level. From first graders to graduate students, I have witnessed the power of this approach to draw students into the learning process and shift from compliant consumers of learning to engaged learners, creators and producers. I created a handbook for students called, *IDEAS: A Simple Guide for Kids to Learn About Anything.*[15] This handbook guides students through the inquiry process and helps them learn about topics of interest to them. You can find resources for IDEAS on my website at drcherylpeterson.com.

There are many opportunities to connect the mind and hand, you just need to start with an idea. Once you have one, you might just CHANGE THE WORLD.

PURPOSE - Change the World

BECAUSE OF 4 students an idea changed their world. They showed me what is possible when we invest time in each other and our ideas. Imagine if we had more days like this where kids were so fired up about learning they couldn't stop working on their ideas.

We all have ideas. Sometimes we bury them because we are too busy or too afraid to fail or we just don't know what to do with it. When you nurture and feed an idea it grows. Imagine what your idea might be able to do if you let it. In what ways might you grow your ideas. How might you CHANGE THE WORLD?

CHANGE THE WORLD
step-by-step

Students need opportunities to connect their mind and their hands. Play with ideas you have for providing more mind-hand connections for students.

PLAY

Mind-hand learning opportunities can change students and teachers. Identify ways you can incorporate mind-hand learning into your lessons.

PRACTICE

Changing the world starts with an idea. Name four students and tell how you might change the world for them. >AND YOU!

PURPOSE

CREATE A LEARNING PLAN

USING IDEAS, students create a learning plan to explore topics of interest to them. Use this guide to create a learning plan for developing your own leadership, teaching, parenting or coaching skills.

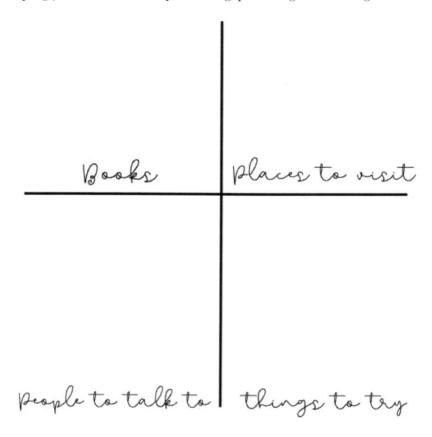

Books | places to visit

people to talk to | things to try

EIGHT

LEADERS

LEAP AND LEAD

Leaders aren't born, they are made. They are made by hard effort, which is the price all of us must pay to achieve any goal which is worthwhile. - Vince Lombardi Jr.[1]

AS I LED the boys back down the hall to their class, they could hardly contain their excitement. They hopped along-side me chattering.

"Did you see how that car went down the hall?"

"Did you get it all recorded?"

"I hope you didn't mess it up."

"When can we see it?"

"Can we do it again?"

"Next time I'm going to put one of those fan things on mine and see if it can go faster."

I offered Mrs. G an apologetic look as I ushered them noisily back into class. She nodded and mouthed, "Wow!" back at me. These were definitely different students than the ones I had picked up an hour earlier.

Later in the day as I walked through the hall, I noticed Rick and Larry with their heads together looking as if they were plotting something. Knowing they should be in reading groups, I approached them. "I thought you guys have reading group right now. What are you working on?"

They barely glanced up and continued talking as they motioned to a piece of paper. "We figured out how to make the cars go faster next time. See, if we put this on here like this, and then turn one of the buttons, it doesn't go in circles." They continued with their plans adding detailed elements with each new idea.

"What about adding the fan, wouldn't that help it go faster?"

"Yeah, but we might have to make it bigger to hold it and then it will be heavier." On and on went the conversation.

I finally managed to find a lull and broke in. "I'm excited you have such great ideas. We can work on it next time, but scholars have to learn lots of things, and right now you need to be scholars in reading." I wanted to encourage their excitement and hopefully transfer it to other areas as well.

Larry looked at me with a puzzled expression, "you mean we gotta be scholars in reading class too? I thought we were just scholars with you."

I smiled, "Larry, being a scholar is not just something you do, it's who you are. You are a scholar now so that means you must work at being one all the time. But the more you work at it, the more it will become a part of you."

"Man, this scholar stuff is going to be a lot of work."

"Yeah, but it's going to be a lot of fun, too. Remember, a scholar works hard and loves learning. When you love something, it's fun and doesn't really seem like hard work."

"Like this, right?" commented Rick.

"Yeah, like this. Now go be scholars in reading and see if that doesn't get easier, too."

I smiled as I walked away thinking about how to maintain this momentum. It turns out I didn't have to wonder for long. By the end of the day, I had a lunch date with Mrs. G to talk about some ideas she had for the class.

Our professional and personal relationship was growing as quickly as my connection with the boys. We had begun to bounce ideas off each other and I looked forward to what she had up her sleeve, even though part of me still hesitated to get in too deep.

———

AS I WALKED DOWN for our lunch date, I heard the boys before I even reached the classroom door.

"It's Dr. Peterson. Get your lunch, quick."

"Slow down boys," laughed Mrs. G. "It's my turn for lunch with Dr. Peterson."

"What?! That's not fair."

"Nope, it's not fair for you, but it's fair for me."

They gave us their best pout face and went off to lunch.

"How would you like to co-teach a lesson with me?" she suggested as we sat down to lunch.

"Sure," I said instantly thinking about how I might get out of it by saying I didn't have time. It was true, I didn't have any extra time and the boys were already taking the few minutes I didn't have to spare. "What do you have in mind?" I asked interested, but still reluctant.

"Well, I want to borrow the Little Bit sets and have the boys lead groups in designing range rovers for the end of our unit on the moon. I thought I would have each of the boys lead a group."

While the boys were certainly enthusiastic and had done a great job building with me, I had a hard time imagining them leading groups. However, I knew it was a great opportunity for them to develop their leadership skills. "Ok, let's do it. We'll work on practicing building the cars and refining some leadership skills. You have a lot of strong personalities in your class. How do you think they are going to handle letting these guys lead?"

"I think it's going to be an adventure," Mrs. G remarked with a smile.

―――――

THE ROOM WAS abuzz with activity when I walked in. In each of the four corners stood a leader. Each of them was leading in their own way.

"It goes like this," commanded Rick as he showed the group exactly how pieces went together.

Larry collaborated with his team members by asking, "What's your idea? What do you think?"

Always the cheerleader, Michael enthusiastically encouraged his team members, "Ok work together guys. We got this," he cheered as he danced around.

"Let's each take a turn, guys," encouraged Jerry, always aware of everyone's feelings and struggling to not get swept up in the group dynamics that sometimes overwhelmed him.

It wasn't an easy class to lead. There were several bright students who liked to take control, but struggled with any task that didn't have clear directions. Some of the students had a lot of energy and just wanted to grab and start doing without working together. But there were four confident boys in the room ready to take on the challenge.

"Look, these pieces are really expensive. You have to be careful and act like a scholar," I overheard one of the boys explaining to his group. It was validating to realize he had heard and was using my phrases. It was also a bit surreal seeing them try to manage a group using many of the same words and actions I had used to manage them.

Each group was given a STEM challenge to meet. Their cars had to meet certain criteria, include certain components and be able to solve a particular challenge problem. The students used language and skills from science, technology, engineering and math in solving the problem. As I looked around the room, one by one, cars were built meeting all the criteria of the STEM challenge. Something else was being built, too. One by one, as each group tackled the challenging task before them, a leader emerged.

PLAY - Leap and Lead

The boys practiced the actions and attitudes of scholars in their small group with me, but until this lesson their opportunities for leadership were limited to the lunchroom and the playground. While confident in their abilities as leaders on the playground, the boys were painfully aware of their limitations in academics. In reading and math, they used a variety of strategies to protect themselves from revealing these weaknesses.

Their reactions all fit within the classic fight, flight or freeze response to fear. All humans, when exposed to a threatening situation, produce chemicals and thinking patterns to prepare them to face the threat. Most reactions can be categorized in one of three responses, fight, flight or freeze.

In the classroom, fight may look like an actual fight of words or fists between students, but it can also be refusal to work or an angry retort to a teacher. Sometimes a student will actually run out of the classroom in flight, but more common reactions are subtle. They include trips to the bathroom, drinking fountain or even to the school nurse. They may just be wandering around the room or sharpening a pencil. Sometimes students just seem to freeze and do nothing. Commonly described as daydreaming, this is one way students disengage in the classroom and respond to fear.

Although we often don't realize it, asking a student to read a paragraph or complete a math problem could be a fear inducing situation. For students who learn differently or who are not as strong in these areas, these situations can be fear inducing and toxic. A far better strategy for propelling students forward is to create an environment where they can utilize their strengths and build on their success.

This was our goal with the lesson. One of the reasons this lesson worked so well was because we flipped some of the learning. Rather than teaching the lesson and then picking up the stragglers with extra lessons and practice, we preloaded the boys with the knowledge and skills they would need to be successful leaders. We already knew they had a natural affinity for leadership and for figuring out the Little Bits. It was the perfect opportunity to purposefully create an environment for them to practice their leadership skills.

———

ACCORDING TO BENJAMIN HARDY,[2] an expert on willpower, one of the common mistakes we make is to think we need to prepare ourselves for roles. In his book, *Willpower Doesn't Work: Discover the Hidden Keys to Success*, he states that to improve, we need to grow into our potential and roles. We grow by setting up environments and situations that challenge us to improve.

So often with students, we spend so much time prepping them and teaching them the skills they will need to do a task that we leave little time for them to perform the task. Actual opportunities to perform are necessary for the skill to develop. It doesn't mean all prep work and supports are ignored. There just needs to be time beyond it for actual practice.

This Little Bits leadership lesson was carefully designed based on our knowledge of the students, the strength areas they brought to the groups, and the outcomes we hoped to achieve. We didn't just randomly create groups. The boys had far more experience and confidence with the Little Bits than their classmates, which gave them an authentic advantage and allowed them to assume the leadership roles we had hoped for them.

This lesson didn't happen by accident, but it wasn't planned like most lessons either. Most lessons are constructed. They start with an objective and then activities are planned to guide students through mastering the desired outcomes. The focus is mainly on what the teacher and students do. Most lessons include some sort of teacher demonstration or instruction, guided practice, independent practice, and assessment.

One of the challenges with lessons and particularly with lessons planned in this way is getting the students to participate in the learning. According to Phil Schlechty in his book *Engaging Students*,[3] the challenge for all educators is engagement. One of the key ideas in Schlechty's work is understanding who we are teaching, what we are asking them to do, and how students are responding to those requests. Schlechty argues much of our time in schools is spent on meaningless activities resulting in three main student reactions: compliance, retreatism and rebellion. However, the goal of lesson design should be engagement.

In response to this challenge, Schlechty suggests a different approach to lesson planning called *design*. This idea comes from work engineers, marketers and other industry experts have been doing around design thinking. *Design thinking*[4] is a creative process where knowledge about the end user and the problem is used to drive the creation of a design. In Schlechty's work, a key component to the design process is being very clear about who your students are and what are their needs.

This lesson wasn't constructed, it was designed. We started with our "who." We purposefully planned for the students in this class based on what we knew about them and what we thought would help them experience the design process themselves and develop skills as leaders. Because of this the students were able to LEAP INTO LEADERSHIP.

PRACTICE - Leap and Lead

Design thinking is slowly making its way into some of the educational jargon and practices of school. In many cases the students are the first to partake in such practices. A recent focus on engineering as a core component to the science standards has resulted in a surge of STEM challenges focused on using the engineering design process to creatively solve problems and generate solutions.

There are many different iterations of this process, but most include some components of asking questions, imagining creative solutions, planning how to create those solutions, creating or building the idea, experimenting, getting feedback and continuing to iterate and refine the solution. Any Google or Pinterest search for STEM will result in a slew of activities presenting a challenge for kids to solve and a list of all the materials and lesson guides you need to do the lesson. However, this is not how I suggest you begin.

As with so many of the ideas presented in this book, you can't teach what you don't know. Let's face it, most of us are great planners and some of us may have some strong creative skills or even engineering tendencies, but we could probably still benefit from doing some design thinking ourselves. The place to start with design thinking is with **YOU**.

―――――

OUR DISTRICT LEADERSHIP team spent many years working with Phil Schlechty, corporate leaders, and educational leaders to delve into the theory and practice of design thinking and how to incorporate it into our work in the schools. Over time and through extensive learning and practice, the district developed its own version of the design process.

This process guides problem solving and decision making from the top of the district leadership to guiding the lesson planning of teachers and is becoming the way students are learning to approach their work as well. In Spring Lake Park Schools, the design process is called *3D Design: Discover, Design, Deliver.*[5] Because of this foundation, Mrs. G and I had the tools, freedom, and encouragement to design lessons and to share the process with our students.

Design thinking begins with a problem, something you want to work better. In our case, we knew we wanted to create an opportunity for the boys to be leaders in a positive way. Here's how we went about designing our lesson with the 3D approach:

- **Discover**: This phase is about gathering inspiration and insight. This might begin with a story or video clip capturing the issue or problem. For us, our inspiration came the day the boys had so much success with the Little Bits cars. We knew they were engaged and successful with it. We also knew they had skills we could leverage to develop their leadership capacity. We knew the boys and the students in the class well. We shared insights about how the boys and various students in the class worked together in different situations and what skills we thought they needed to develop. We looked at the science curriculum for insight as to how the Little Bits might satisfy the science standards and goals.
- **Design**: There are two components to this phase, *ideate and prototype*. Basically, it's generating ideas and developing them into practice or a model as quickly as possible. It's a cycle of ideating and prototyping continuously informed by

feedback from the user. We brainstormed lots of ideas, finally landing on the idea to do a STEM based activity. Connecting with the science curriculum, students would design range rovers using the Little Bits to confront some of the challenges of navigating the moon's surface. Students would identify a characteristic of the moon's surface that is difficult to navigate and design a range rover to travel over the surface.

- **Deliver**: In this phase, a design is implemented and sometimes refined. This might be teaching a lesson, but it could also be sharing a strategy about how to make the morning routine go smoother. We delivered our design by presenting a lesson to the students and then reflecting on the experience, identifying areas for further teaching, and noting ways we could improve this experience in future lessons or in repeating this lesson with another class.

———

DON'T WAIT until you have all the skills you need to lead with design thinking. Sometimes leading is taking a leap of faith and then gaining the skills you need to along the way. This is something I learned from Mrs. G. I wait. I often procrastinate. I tend to think I will do it someday or I need to learn the right skills first. Mrs. G taught me to leap and lead.

The boys needed an opportunity to bring their success beyond the walls of my little, small group room and to build on their success. If we would have waited for the exact right time to do this lesson or until I had spent more time learning about the Little Bits and finding the perfect way to introduce the lesson, the opportunity would have been missed.

Similarly, my district pushed me to lead with design thinking. I wasn't an expert by any means at using the design process, but my charge as a leader was not to learn it completely and then do it; rather it was to start experimenting with the process and lean into it.

Are you waiting to be a leader? Are you waiting to build your students into leaders? It's time to stop waiting and start moving. **LEAP AND LEAD**!

PURPOSE - Leap and Lead

BECAUSE OF 4 students, I experienced how important it is to leap and lead. You don't have to wait until you have all the skills you need to do something or to be a leader. Sometimes leading is taking a leap of faith and then gaining the skills you need along the way. Planning and preparation are important but can be a perfection trap. Opportunities are missed when we fail to commit until we have a perfect plan, or we spend too much time learning and not enough time doing.

What's holding you back? You might fail, it's true. But if you fail forward, you can build on that failure and turn it into a success. If you do nothing, you fail to push yourself to develop new skills and to develop abilities you need to confront new challenges. We all fail. It's just a matter of how we fail and what we do next that counts. Don't wait to be the leader your students deserve. Don't wait to see the leadership potential in them. Every moment spent waiting is a wasted opportunity. In what ways might you **LEAP AND LEAD**?

LEAP AND LEAD
step-by-step

Lesson design begins with understanding the who, the student.
Play with ideas you have for understanding the strengths and needs
of your learners.

PLAY

3D Design is a process for creating solutions.
Discover, Design and Deliver a solution to a problem you or your
learners face.

PRACTICE

Designing a new experience might require you to leap and lead
Name four students and tell how you might
leap and lead them. >AND YOU!

PURPOSE

NINE

PLANS

DREAM BIG

---

*With great power, there must also come, great responsibility. -Marvel
Comics, Spider-Man*[1]

MY CLASSROOM space sometimes felt like a balloon, expanding to hold whatever was put in it. In all actuality, it was about a 12 by 12-foot space. I managed to fit a file cabinet and enough shelves to hold all the enrichment materials I used and shared with teachers. I chose to fit three tables with chairs instead of the large metal teacher's desk. I could work with groups of 12 kids at a time in my room. I had learned to work almost anywhere with my groups, including hallways and storage closets, so having an actual room felt like a luxury.

On this day, however, my balloon classroom felt as if it were about to pop! Several teachers joined me in my space for a design day. We were excited to have a dedicated day to design lessons to engage all students and focus on bringing in some extension activities to support our high achieving students.

Teachers carry around a lot of stuff; books, supplies, worries, and aspirations. Today was no different. In addition to the piles of curriculum resources and materials, data, and snacks, hung our hopes and fears. We knew we weren't reaching some of our students. Some were so far behind in skills we didn't know where to begin. Others were so far ahead we didn't know how to keep from holding them back. Some parents were so actively involved we felt smothered, while others failed to engage no matter what we tried.

The seasons were changing, growing colder, and we had been faced with numerous days of indoor recess and the concern about improving test scores in the spring. But we knew this day was a gift. We had a day to work together to design learning opportunities for our students.

———

ARMED WITH COFFEE AND CHOCOLATE, we were ready to dig in. Energy and enthusiasm were high. There was a quiet hum in the room as everyone worked on their piles. Suddenly, Mrs. G broke the silence. "I wish I could do something with all of my students to meet them at their levels, but let them work together, too. I feel like we separate them so much by ability, but they can also learn from common experiences. If they could learn to work together better, we could also use that to support their learning in lots of areas."

"That sounds like a design question to me," I commented. The teachers recently attended a workshop on design thinking, and I knew this was a great opportunity to apply it to our work, so I rephrased her comment into the language of design thinking. "In what ways might we provide opportunities for our students to learn at their level and work together toward a common goal? Let's start with our 'who.' What do we know about our students?"

"There's the group of high-achieving readers. They need something at a high level, but they really struggle with some of their group skills. They want to put in their own ideas without listening to anyone else."

"And then there are the four boys I work with, and some of your lower students. They don't want anyone to see them read, but we saw with the land rover lesson how well they can lead a group. But they don't really have the confidence to use this strength with academic challenges."

"Yep, and both groups really need physical movement with their learning. They like to get their hands-on things to understand it."

"Ok, so we have a pretty good idea of our who, and what really is our desired outcome?"

"You know, neither group enjoys the reading materials, so they aren't really spending much time reading. I'd like to get them excited about a topic and read. So, motivation is a desired outcome for me. I'd also like them to develop some skills in working together. As a group, their collaboration skills are really lacking. If they are going to move forward in their skills, they need to be excited about reading and be able to learn and work together."

"It sounds like we are looking for something to encourage reading, pull students together in groups, and provide some opportunities to work with their hands as well as their minds." As I summarized our thinking out loud, I realized the tall order we were envisioning.

"What kinds of things besides the Little Bits have they been enjoying with you?" asked Mrs. G.

"They really like the Keva[2] blocks. I challenged them to build as tall of a structure as they could the other day. You should have seen the ideas they came up with to make them stronger and higher."

"Hmmm.... what about a gingerbread literature unit? We can combine it with a concluding STEM activity. The kids could use the blocks to build a structure to protect the gingerbread man from a winter snowstorm. We could teach it on the day before winter break."

"Great idea," I said, secretly thinking she was crazy. The day before winter break? The boys were better with school, but that day was always tough even for the less-challenging students. Some kids were excited about the upcoming holidays while others were full of fear and dread. But I didn't have any groups the day before winter break, and I could help. I drummed up a little more enthusiasm. "Let's do it," I said. "Let's go back to our design question and see if this helps answer it."

"We wanted to make sure we could engage the students at different levels. I think I can drum up some enthusiasm for reading if I connect it to a fun building activity at the end. We can gather various gingerbread stories at different reading levels. We can also plan time for small group creative writing work."

"We also want to support the students in working collaboratively. I'll work with the gifted kids and the boys on some language they can use to communicate their ideas. That way most of your class will have some practice and vocabulary."

We continued to iron out the details and make sure we were addressing the skills we wanted students to develop and paying special attention to some students we knew would need some extra support. Our day flew by quickly as I continued to work with Mrs. G and the other teachers. They were now inspired by our idea to dig in to designing their own lessons. One by one, ideas and energy flowed into the room. Just as the balloon was filled, I knew I had to share my personal news.

———

"IT LOOKS like we are at about the end of our day and need to wrap things up. I'm really excited about all the lessons we designed today, and I can't wait to see all of them in action. Before we break for today though, I have some news I need to share."

I took a deep breath and let go of the balloon. "You may know my husband has been out of work. Well, he took a job out of state. He's been out there since September. I'm going to stay until spring break and then join him."

The balloon shot around the room releasing its air. It felt as if everyone at once sucked in all the air and the balloon lay deflated on the floor.

PLAY - Dream Big

Why does it so often feel like there is never enough? Enough time? Money? Patience? In teaching, I worry about the kids who struggle and how they and I will be measured at the end of the day. At home I worry about getting dinner on the table, papers signed, and the kids doing the right things. I worry about how everything looks to everyone else. Time is my scapegoat.

This all began to change for me during a design training exercise. I was working with other district leaders to learn how to design by doing the process ourselves. As my group worked through brainstorming solutions to our problem, we kept stopping ourselves with deficit thinking: "there's no time" and "there's no money." The leader stopped us and said, "time can't be an excuse. We all get 24 hours, so it's a matter of how you prioritize that time."

I remember being angry at this statement. That's easy for him to say I thought, but I have an impossible task list, my husband is living in a different state. I'm barely able to get kids to practice let alone have time for additional schoolwork. He doesn't get how hard teachers work. He isn't in my shoes. I yelled LOUDLY to no one. But the idea continued to fester in me.

I started thinking more and more about time and how I was using my time. As my colleagues and I began to use design thinking more and more, we began to solve more and more problems. We found ways to bend or move time to better fit our priorities. We got creative with what we could do and when. We played with time. We found ways to weave great ideas into our teaching and we somehow found the time. Often our solutions took far less time than we had spent complaining about our "lack of."

THE DEFICIT MODEL we hold about time and resources is similar to the one we often hold for our students. When we focus on what we don't have, it is more difficult to recognize opportunities not just of time and resources, but for our students. Shifting this mindset isn't easy. For me it takes recognizing when the words, "I have to," enter my mind and shifting them to "I want to, I get to, I choose to." It also means making an effort to express gratitude rather than a complaint.

One of the initiatives proposed by my leadership team after reading, *The Fred Factor,*[3] was to write thank you notes. We decided to write five thank you notes a week to other colleagues or any other district employee who impacted us and to share specific feedback about their actions. As great as this idea sounded, I often struggled to find the time to write my notes. Over time, as I focused more on gratitude, I found not only did the notes come easier but so did the moments of time I needed to write them.

———

FULFILLING DREAMS CAN SEEM a daunting task if you focus on deficits. I'll never have enough time or resources to do everything. I need to plan and prioritize to reach my goals. I have a coffee cup I use daily to remind me of this. Written on it are the words, Dream BIG, Start SMALL, Act Now. This captures the essence of designing learning opportunities and limiting deficit thinking.

The combination of these three ideas is the key. Sometimes failure occurs because too much time is spent dreaming. Visioning desired outcomes is necessary, but without action and usually some hard work, dreams fall flat.

Perfectionism loves to keep us stuck in a dream state. If it can keep us focused on wanting rather than acting, it can keep us from growing. Perfectionism hates growing. It wants you to keep things safe and predictable. To break the hold of perfectionism, you need to start small. Small actionable goals are easier to act on and gain momentum.

Then all you need to do is take that next step again and again and again. Don't have enough? Use what you do have and start dreaming and doing. DREAM **BIG,** start small and act now.

PRACTICE - Dream Big

You may think constraints limit your ability to dream big, but constraints can be good for innovation. According to the *Harvard Business Review*,[4] "constraints provide focus and a creative challenge that motivate people to search for and connect information from different sources to generate novel ideas for new products, services, or (business) processes."

One of the most debilitating phrases in the teacher's language is, "We have to…" Every teacher knows how to finish this sentence. We have to teach these standards; we have to get our test scores up; we have to teach math at 1:00; we have to ability-group for reading and math. Fill in the blank with whatever "have to," you think you have. Every teacher has a list of "have to's." Parents and coaches have similar "have to's" also.

——————

BUT WHAT IF this weren't true? What if this was just a story you tell yourself? Often complaints about these "have to's" serve as a pretty good excuse for failing to meet desired goals. You might want to teach a great lesson on the civil war, but you have to follow the state standards and it's not taught at your grade level. You might want to spend more time on writing, but you have to make sure students are ready for the standardized test, so you can't afford the time.

These stories work very well for keeping us at the status quo. I think the status quo has become an acceptable level in education. But what if I told you there were very simple changes in wording to turn this thinking around and begin to change everything, including how much energy you have available. Would you take it?

"I get to, I want to, I choose to…" Replacing the "have to," phrase with one of these phrases creates a huge shift in focus and expectations. There are lots of things you have to do, but you also "get to" teach students. You "get to," impact a life in a meaningful and impactful way.

As teachers, parents, and coaches, we have an enormous amount of power. If you doubt that, just think about something you have achieved in your life. I bet a teacher, parent or coach either encouraged you or created a poor learning experience, forcing you to take a stand and rise above it. We owe much of our learning in life to a *teacher* whether it's from a parent, another person or life itself.

———

I ONCE STOOD at a training for teachers in which the whole room felt deflated because our test scores didn't measure up. We didn't meet our "have to" goals. However, we weren't just teaching what was being measured on the test. We were teaching students be good citizens, to believe in themselves, to work hard and persist. We were teaching our students to collaborate and solve problems creatively.

On these measures, we had countless pieces of evidence demonstrating our success. We could name students who started the year with no self-control able to persist on an extended reading task. We had students who could not self-regulate their behaviors and outbursts now able to work cooperatively with others. We started with a new and fairly disjointed staff and came together as a team to create a cardboard golf course filling an entire gym.

If we measured students by numbers and correct answers on a multiple-choice test, we failed. But if we measured our students by how much they had grown and developed their strengths, we were a huge success. We still "have to" address those other areas, but if we "choose to" build on our successes and strengths rather than our perceived failures we gain much more.

———

SHIFTING mindset is the first step toward being able to design learning opportunities for students. As teachers, parents, and coaches, it is important to stop thinking about what *has* to be done and start thinking about what opportunities exist for our students to help them move forward. One way is to rephrase obstacles with the phrase "How might we…" In this provocation for example, rather than continuing to focus on the problem of students being at so many different levels, we chose to look for opportunities related to this problem.

This phrase can cause quite a reaction as it first gets worked into a culture. I remember getting so frustrated when I posed a problem to my supervisor. I wanted her to see the problem and fix it. I remember sharing with her that I couldn't do the literature unit I had planned because we didn't have enough books. I wanted to purchase more books. Rather than simply approving my request, she turned the problem into a "how might we…" opportunity. "How might we give the students an enriched reading experience?" she asked.

We brainstormed and ended up using several different novels and having students discuss the ideas from the books rather than the content of the book itself. The designed lesson was a better learning experience than I would have provided if I had just ordered the books. But this shift is not easy to make and can raise quite a few tensions and conflicts.

We can choose to take a positive approach and look for opportunities rather than obstacles. In my experience in doing design work with teachers, this mindset shift can get the process started, but two pitfalls often sabotage even the best forward thinking: the *false start* and *perfection paralysis*.

———

THERE ARE lots of places to get great ideas for lessons and tons of resources. There are prepackaged curriculum materials, teacher lesson guides, free lessons on the internet, Teachers pay Teachers website, and Pinterest. If you want an activity or lesson to do with students, there is no shortage of ready resources. This is a false start.

The place to begin is not figuring out what you want to do, but who you are designing the lesson for and identify a targeted learning objective:

- what you want them to know
- what they should understand and
- what they should be able to do (i.e., targeted learning objective).

When teachers focus on the lesson they are going to teach, their planning focuses on what they are going to do and how they are going to do it. Lessons deliver content and assume the student will absorb it. However, it doesn't foster deep and meaningful learning. It must be experienced by the student. **The best a teacher can do is create the environment and conditions for learning to occur.** Therefore, it is important for teachers to stop teaching lessons and start designing effective learning opportunities for students.

———

ONE OF THE best resources I have found for doing this comes from the work of Phil Schlechty. One of the first steps in Schlechty's design process, which was illustrated in this provocation, is to begin with the who. In this critical first step, you identify the unique attributes and qualities of the learner. Much like designers do in creating an innovative product, you start by developing a "spec" sheet clearly describing your end user.

From there, Schlechty describes ten elements necessary for designing engaging work. Full descriptions of these elements and planning templates are available at the Schlechty Center website.[5] Rather than define and explain each of these here, I will demonstrate how the learning opportunity Mrs. G and I designed met these design elements.

- **Content and Substance** – These are the essential learnings students must master. For our purpose, this was working cooperatively in a group, writing a creative story, and reading a variety of texts.
- **Product Focus** – In coming up with the gingerbread idea, our final product focus was a collection of creative stories and a group-based STEM competition to build structures for the gingerbread men.
- **Organization of Knowledge** – We identified a variety of texts at different levels so students could read creative stories about gingerbread men, as well as information at their reading level. Students were provided instruction and supports for creative writing. Students were also taught language to help support group collaboration.
- **Clear and Compelling Product Standards** – We identified and shared criteria with students for how they needed to work in their collaborative group, the goals of the block structure, and the reading and writing goals.
- **Protection from Adverse Consequences for Initial Failures** – The activity was set in a fun atmosphere in which students had multiple opportunities to revise their structure designs.
- **Affiliation** – The students participated in determining the focus of the creative gingerbread stories and developed the goals with the teacher.
- **Affirmation** – The gingerbread stories were shared with the kindergarten buddy class. Sharing a product or process affirms the importance of the learning.
- **Choice** – Students were able to assign participant roles and design their structures in any way using the blocks provided. They were also given choices of books to read and writing prompts and styles.

- **Novelty and Variety** – The activities in this learning opportunity were much different and involved different groupings of students than was the norm for their reading instruction.
- **Authenticity** – Students were able to create and build to solve a proposed problem and to read books related to the theme of the activity. It was authentic because the activity connected with their learning and potential real life experiences.

The dreams we had for the students were big, but we were off to a good start with understanding our who and making plans based on our students first and then focusing on our content goals.

The next trap we needed to avoid was perfection paralysis. This one is sneaky. This is the one that finds holes or problems with everything you are trying to do so you won't start in the first place. Remember my perfection paralysis responses, "it's the day before winter break, they won't be able to lead, there's too many different needs in the class." If I had continued down that path rather than stuck with Mrs. G's moment, this lesson never would have happened. Don't let perfection paralysis stop your big dreams. DREAM **BIG,** start small, act now.

PURPOSE - Dream Big

BECAUSE OF **4** students, we dreamt big, started small and acted. When we put students in the forefront of the lesson planning, we were able to create an impactful learning experience to meet the students' needs and the learning outcomes. We had big dreams for the students, and they rose to our expectations.

Don't be left with empty dreams because you failed to act or reach your potential because you didn't dream big enough. Put perfectionism to rest and dream big. The first step is the hardest but start. Start small. Hesitation opens the door for perfectionism to grab hold so don't wait. How might you DREAM **BIG,** start small and act now?

DREAM BIG
step-by-step

Dreaming big begins with focusing on gratitude and abundance rather than deficits. Play with dreams you have and ideas for expressing gratitude.

PLAY

False starts and perfection paralysis can sabotage your dreams. Identify actions you can take to avoid these pitfalls and create opportunities.

PRACTICE

Achieving big dreams depends on small steps and consistent action. Name four students and tell how you might dream big for them. >AND YOU!

PURPOSE

CREATE A DREAM SCAFFOLD

Big dreams require a solid foundation. Think about a dream you have for yourself or your children, students or players. Identify elements you can use to support the dream and build a foundation for it to grow.

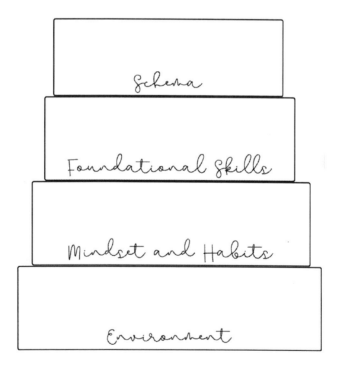

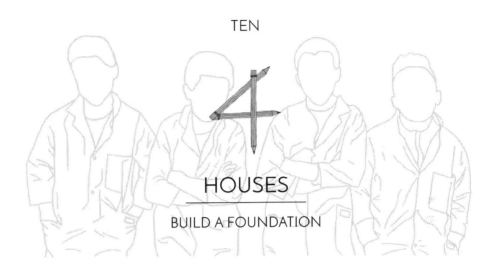

TEN

HOUSES

BUILD A FOUNDATION

You must expect great things of yourself before you can do them. -
Michael Jordan[1]

IT WAS the day before winter break. No visions of sugar plums danced in the students' heads. In Mrs. G's room, gingerbread was the only thing on everyone's mind. For the last few weeks, the students in Mrs. G's class focused on meeting the reading standards with stories about the Gingerbread Man. They worked hard on their reading and writing for the promise of an exciting activity. Creative stories written by the students adorned the hallway outside of the class. Inside, the long-anticipated activity was commencing.

The afternoon before winter break can be a challenging day. Some students are excited about their plans for vacation or time with family, while others are filled with anxiety and worry about the conflicts that occur when families collide, spending time with unfamiliar guests or relatives, and the stress of strained finances. The extra activities during the holidays leave some students tired and stressed. However, no one in Mrs. G's class was thinking about the upcoming break. I could feel the charge in the air the second I walked into the classroom.

———

ALTHOUGH MY ENTRANCE usually drew a lot of attention, today I was barely noticed. There was a buzz. Not a bad kind of buzz, but the kind of buzz where you just know kids are active and engaged. It's not exactly loud and chaotic, but it's not quiet either. Five distinct groups of kids were spread out around the room. Each group huddled around a cluster of desks pushed together for the activity. Piled near or on the desks were bags of Keva[2] blocks. Students were working together to create a structure.

"We're ready!" shouted one group.

"Ok, here is your gingerbread man," Mrs. G exclaimed as she handed the group a gingerbread cookie. "Go ahead and place it inside your structure. Then we'll see if it can withstand the snow-storm." Mrs. G had an animated grin on her face and was holding 2 bags of powder sugar. The students placed their gingerbread man inside the structure.

"Ready?" said Mrs. G in a jovial tone, a huge smile on her face.

"Ready!" the team shouted in unison.

As she placed the bags on the structure, the students began count-ing, "1...2...3...4...5...6...7...8...9...10.... YEAH!!!!," cheers erupted like an explosion. "We did it! It worked!"

———

AROUND THE ROOM a similar scene was happening in every group. Kids were working together, challenging each other, trying different things. In many ways, there was nothing unique about this. I've seen lots of teachers do STEM activities with a similar look and feel. Usually students are engaged and excited, working together on a problem in groups. A casual observer who didn't know the class might not even take a second glance.

But I did know this class. I knew there were 8 students with high academic abilities. According to most conventional standards, they were considered in the gifted to highly gifted range. Each of these students had a very strong personality and didn't like to make mistakes or to be wrong. Some of them could be very emotional, prone to crying or angry outbursts. Most of them were also vocal and would not hesitate to give their opinion and insist any other way was wrong.

Right beside these gifted kids were others of average ability and kids with lower abilities in reading and writing. There were unique talents and needs in each of them. And then there were the four boys: Rick, Larry, Michael, and Jerry. Over the last few months, we had bonded. But even though we had great moments together, their daily moods and attitudes could sometimes derail the best laid plans like a rock laid on a railroad track.

———

I BLINKED IN SURPRISE, holding back a small tear of pride. Michael, who never stopped moving was bouncing a few steps back from the desk clusters trying to make sure he didn't bump the table. "You can do it, Sarah!" Don't give up. You have a great idea," he encouraged as his team members built a structure in response to his cheerful directions.

Rick, who usually stared down his competition until they backed off, was head-to-head in deep conversation with Harry, one of the brightest in the class.

"What way do you think we should lay this next layer so it's stronger?" asked Harry.

"If we stack them like this, it's much stronger. My tower last week held a book," replied Rick with confidence and authority in his voice.

Over in Larry's corner, he practiced much of the language we talked about in class. Using this language and his natural leadership abilities, Larry focused on getting consensus from everyone in his group and encouraged them to make a group decision. "Sarah, you haven't shared an idea yet, what do you think?" I overheard him saying.

"I'm not sure. I think maybe we should turn the blocks this way so it's taller," replied Sarah with uncertainty.

I could tell he knew it was a bad idea, but rather than try to be a hero himself, Larry, kept up the leadership role. "Why don't we try your idea and see if it works? It's ok if it doesn't, then we'll know what doesn't work."

Not too far away in another corner Jerry's group already had a structure built. Jerry and Mike worked side by side, carefully placing the gingerbread man inside the structure so they could perform the final snow test. Jerry, sometimes overwhelmed by the classroom activity, was in control of himself and the group. "Ok guys, we got this! Let's be really careful now as we put this in. We don't want it to fall apart now."

———

OVER THE NEXT HOUR, the activity and the day wrapped up with an air of excitement and energy. No drama, no fights, no fussing at how it wasn't their fault in the principal's office.

"Can we try to add more weight?"

"Do you think we could make it with less bricks?"

"I bet we could do it this way"

The phrases circled around the room as the students continued to build, test, and build again. When the bell rang at the end of the day, Mrs. G's class, known to end like a dropped box of pots and pans, clattering and scattering into the hallway, sounded more like a symphony. Although it might have been a little loud with a few missed notes here and there, her class played some beautiful music. Conversations continued as the students poured into the hall to head for their buses and the start of winter break.

"Did you see how tall we got ours?"

"Can you believe it didn't break even after 20 seconds?"

PLAY - Build a Foundation

Run, run as fast as you can. You can't catch me, I'm the Gingerbread Man.[3] But the sly fox does catch the Gingerbread Man, by convincing him he isn't a hungry fox but a way over the river. The gingerbread man never had a chance. The fox didn't want him to succeed, he set him up to fail. A sly fox doesn't provide a firm foundation for crossing a river.

Unfortunately, we pull this sleight of hand on children and students all the time. I know I do. Here's how it happens. I'll tell my kids to clean up without ever really teaching them or being specific about what that means and then I'm angry when things aren't done the way I expected.

As a parent, I've been frustrated helping my children prepare for exams. When they get to the end of a unit, I often ask them what they are supposed to study for a test. Time and time again, they get to this point and have no clue. Perhaps part of the problem is that they are missing key foundational skills.

Another part is the way we sometimes teach students. We dish out little pieces at a time. Learn this fact. *Climb on my back says the fox.* Learn that fact. *Climb on my head says the fox.* And so on, and so on until, **snap**! There's a test tomorrow, put all the pieces together now.

————

ENGAGED and empowered learning requires a firm foundation. Building a firm foundation includes creating an enriching environment, developing mindset and habits, supporting foundational skills and schema. Let's break each of these down.

Environment

The environment you create can have a large influence on your success or failure. The environment includes all the things surrounding you and your ability to think and focus on learning. Some environments are stimulating and encouraging while others can be stifling. The color, lighting, temperature, and seating can all influence the environment. But there also some more subtle aspects to the environment like how it is organized or the visual stimulants that are displayed.

Think about the example of my kids picking up their room. If everything was organized and had a place or I had a picture of what a clean room looked like, it would be much easier for my children to complete the task successfully. If their teachers posted daily learning targets or visuals related to the unit, perhaps they might have a better idea of the topic and what's important to study and learn.

Mindsets and Habits

The mindset you have toward learning and the habits you develop to support it are critical foundational skills. Carol Dweck[4] has done some of the most extensive research on this area. She emphasizes your mindsets are often related to an activity.

For example, my son may have a fixed mindset toward room cleaning. This is the attitude that no amount of effort will change the outcome. Because of this mindset, he may feel he will never be able to clean his room to my specifications and therefore, why bother?

My daughter may have a growth mindset toward her algebra class. With a growth mindset she believes she can grow and learn with sustained, intentional effort. With this mindset she might begin to take better notes or ask for an outline at the start of a unit to help her better organize and prepare for the final test. She might do practice activities and continue to develop her under-standing.

Habits are also a part of this foundation. They are the things you do automatically without thinking. You may have bad habits such as leaving out dishes or not completing homework, but you can also establish good habits to bring you closer to your desired goals. Chapter 3 discussed the *Habits of Mind*[5] which are great habits to introduce to students. They help establish a common vocabulary, norms, and ways of learning.

Foundational Skills

These are the skills students need to be able to do a task. My son may need instructions on how to run the washing machine. My daughter may need some basic algebra skills, note taking, and study skills to be able to effectively prepare for a test. Often when there is a challenge with learning, there is a good chance some of the foundational skills are lacking.

Schema

Finally, schema...the most important of them all! I must write this for all my grad school friends. I will never forget our lectures on *Schema Theory* by Michael Graves at the University of Minnesota. He was so adamant about it being the foundation of all learning. We had many great discussions and readings on this topic.

Basically, schema is the way ideas, thoughts and concepts are organized. This is so foundational because many disciplines have a schema already developed. Think about grammar and all the rules and structures. Another example of schema is the way animals are classified in biology.

The challenge is even young children have schemas about how the world works and how it is organized. Often their schemas are vastly different from those taught in school. In my previous examples, my schema for a clean room is one where clothes are folded in drawers and beds are made. My son's schema is one where clothes are tossed on the bed and blankets are on the floor. As my daughter studies for her math test, her only schema is the problem she completed for homework. She hasn't connected them to the larger concepts or structure of math.

In sports, players need to transfer the skills of practice to the schema of playing a game. As teachers, parents and coaches, the best thing we can do to set a solid foundation is to share with students the schema and give them opportunities to share and connect their schemas. When we connect ideas, we learn. This connection is part of building our schema and it's a lifelong process.

———

IN THE DESIGN process for the gingerbread lesson, we carefully considered the students and our goals for the learning opportunity. Although we were worried about energy levels being too high or low right before winter break, we built a foundation for success. Success wasn't the surprise. The surprise surfaced in how this foundation created a shift in student roles.

You could almost see students looking at each other with new eyes as they realized who had skills at building and who didn't. Some students were disappointed by their own lack of skill and tried to learn by watching others. Other students were amazed and quickly gained confidence matching their ability. All of this was possible because we **BUILT A FOUNDATION**.

PRACTICE - Build a Foundation

Just around the time of this lesson, we were starting to make plans to relocate to our new home. After returning from a house hunting trip, I curled up in the closet and cried. This had been our home and our firm foundation. We had friends and a support structure. I loved my job, my friends and my community.

Part of establishing a firm foundation for students is having one ourselves. Teaching, parenting, and coaching are tough jobs. To do them, you need a tribe. I was so afraid of losing my foundation, but when we did eventually move, I learned how adaptable I could be and how I could continue to grow and stretch even when I was in unfamiliar territory.

———

TECHNOLOGY HAS ALLOWED many opportunities to continue to build collaborative experiences. It turned out to be a tremendous benefit when we finally moved. I was able to do parts of my job remotely for almost two years. I was also able to stay in contact with the students and colleagues and, of course, my friends.

Connecting in today's digital world has never been more difficult or promising. On the one hand, many of today's social media platforms suck us into a time trap and spur meaningless, superficial relationships. There are many educators, however, who are using these platforms to connect and collaborate in ways which were not previously possible.

I joined the Innovative Teaching Academy,[6] an online course and platform developed by A.J. Juliani. I followed his blog and writing for some time and was intrigued by the idea. My comfort level with signing up for a course like this initially focused on the course cost and lack of educational credits. But I decided to leap and try it.

The course far exceeded my expectations. Not only did I begin to learn and develop skills related to writing and innovation, I also gained a community. The thinking and sharing within this group challenged me to higher levels than I ever considered possible.

I connected with people across the world as well as some I didn't know existed in my own backyard. I even secured an interview because of a connection within the class. I had no idea at the time that this was only a taste of what would soon happen to the entire world.

In 2020 because of the COVID-19 pandemic, almost the entire world was pushed into this digital and sometimes isolated existence. During this time, A.J. Juliani developed many resources and supports for teachers.

———

THERE ARE many on-line learning communities and courses to support almost any area of personal growth and connecting with others with similar or even diverse interests. The COVID-19 pandemic increased the availability of on-line options as well. As with any consumption of goods or services, it is important to be an informed and critical consumer.

Just as there are good courses and programs, some won't be right for you or deliver what you need at the level you need it. Be sure to do your homework. Most reputable programs offer some free materials so you can get a sense of their worth before diving in and provide a money back guarantee. Don't be lured by great promises. The best any of these programs can do is create an environment for you to connect and grow. You still must do the work and build your own foundation.

The bottom line is, to build anything, whether it is a classroom of learners, a happy family, or a life you love, you need a solid foundation. Building one requires teamwork and collaboration. You need a tribe for celebrating the wins and supporting you through the losses. When we have what we need as teachers and parents, it's easier to set up a solid foundation for our students and kids. It's ok to take care of yourself first. You're going to need it. Don't be fooled by the sly fox...**BUILD A FOUNDATION.**

PURPOSE - Build a Foundation

BECAUSE OF 4 students I built a firm foundation, and they grew their leadership capacity. After weeks of practice, they demonstrated their leadership skills in ways I never could have predicted. As teachers, parents, and coaches, we need to take chances with our lessons and our students to push ourselves and them beyond the limits of our comfort zones. But we also need to lay firm foundations for students to be successful.

The environment, mindsets and habits, foundational skills and schema are all essential components to building a firm foundation. But most important is having a solid foundation for yourself. Surround yourself with a collaborative community of friends and colleagues who can challenge and support you. You've got this. Get a team and **BUILD A FOUNDATION.**

BUILD A FOUNDATION
step-by-step

A foundation includes the environment, mindset, habits, skills and schema. Play with ideas you have for strengthening these elements with your students.

PLAY

Building a foundation begins with you.
Identify things you can do to firm up your own foundation.

PRACTICE

Success is built on a firm foundation. Name 4 students and tell what you can do to build a foundation for them. >AND YOU!

PURPOSE

ELEVEN

4

WEEKS

BE GRITTY!

'Tis better to have loved and lost, than never to have loved at all. -Alfred Tennyson[1]

"I NEED to tell you guys something and you are going to be mad at me. I just want you to try to listen to the whole thing." My stomach was in knots as I set the boys up for the tough news I had to share.

"What, you're not going to take us anymore? You don't want to teach us?"

No! I screamed silently to myself. After all this time, how could they not see. Why were they so quick to think they weren't wanted? Oh, how I did want them! They had become more than a responsibility; they were my boys. Somewhere along the way my heart opened and like a balloon filling with air, they had pushed it to its limits. I knew from the beginning, this day would come, but I didn't fully grasp how it would feel. I tried to buffer the blow for them. "You are still going to come to these groups. You belong here. You are scholars."

You could cut the tension in the room like a knife. We were all bracing ourselves for what was coming next, but at this point, I held all the cards. I played my ace and was just hoping for a winning hand. It wasn't any use bluffing; these guys could detect a lie a mile away. It was time to just rip the band-aid off and give them the whole thing.

———

"THE ONLY PROBLEM is that I'm moving, and I won't be your teacher."

"WHAT?!"

Their words weren't the only things swirling around the room. Like the temperature change before a tornado, you could feel the energy swirling around the room. Larry jumped up and pushed his chair in hard.

"No, uh-uh, this can't be happening!"

His words burned deep in my soul, and I echoed the thought. I didn't have a choice though. Since September my husband had been living in another state. My own kids had pushed through the school year, knowing they would be ending their year in a new school. I had until spring break. It had once seemed so far away, but now it was right around the corner. Time was not in our favor, and I didn't want to waste a moment of what we had left, but they were still processing the news.

"Can we still come to this room? Who's going to be the teacher?"

"Miss W. is going to be the teacher." I knew they would love her if they gave her a chance. She was the perfect replacement. She had a gentle heart and part of her job was flexible so she could take over my groups. I was ready to talk her up, but before I could get the words out, I was ambushed.

"Who's that?"

"No way! I'm not going with her!"

"Her breath stinks."

"I'm sure she is just mean."

If my heart wasn't so broken, I might have let out a chuckle. Really? Saying her breath stinks was the best they could do? They were already starting the process of pushing me away, but I wasn't about to let them go that easily. We had worked so hard. All of us had opened up and given more than we ever had. There had to be some way to make it worth it.

———

"LOOK GUYS, you don't have to come to these groups, but I want to stay in touch with you. I want to be able to connect with you on Skype and Flipgrid and send letters to you. If you don't come to these groups, it's not going to be easy to do that," I consoled.

They didn't want my consolation prize any more than I did. We ate lunch together, but instead of begging to stay, they quickly finished and asked to go outside. I knew the steam boiling up inside of them needed to be released.

I stood at the window and watched them try to outrun their anger and hurt. I hated being the one to do this to them. Was it wrong to have cared so much? Was I just another notch in the belt of people who had let them down? I blinked back tears, wondering silently where this path would lead and what obstacles might face me on this journey.

PLAY - Be Gritty!

Sometimes events seem to unfold like a perfect storm. You usually don't realize when the first drop hit. The first drop in this story occurred way before I met the four boys. Looking back, it probably explains why I opened my heart and the events unfolded as they did.

Years ago, I was teaching third grade when I met David. David was a new student in the school. He was the smallest boy in the class, but it wasn't the only reason he stood out. He had a rough start in life. He was born to a coke addict and was a foster child. Because of his exposure to drugs before birth, he was a mess without medication. He would bounce around the classroom like a pinball. He drove me crazy. But there was something I loved about him.

At the time, I was beginning to consider adoption to build my own family, so I was reading a lot about drug addiction and attachment issues. I could tell David probably had problems related to both. I was determined to believe in him until he could believe in himself. I began telling David I believed in him, and I knew he was capable of greatness. I went out to recess with him and helped him navigate the playground. I encouraged him whenever I could.

At one point, David and I developed a contract to work on some particularly difficult behaviors. When David met his contract, I told him how proud I was of him and asked if there was something he would like as a reward. I expected to be shelling out a pack of M&M's or no homework passes, but his answer changed my trajectory as a teacher.

Drip.

Drop.

———

"I'D LIKE a blue backpack with a brown bottom."

"Ok, David, I'll see what I can do about that. I'm really proud of you." I said dismissing him off to gym. It was the end of the day, and I had a few minutes in the room to myself. I was surprised by his request, sort of. As I thought about it, I realized David was the only student in my class who did not have a backpack. He carried a black messenger bag, the kind you get for free at a conference. I don't know why it never occurred to me it might bother him.

I also wondered about the specifics of his request. It made me think there must be someone in our class whom he admired. I scoured the hallway hooks, looking at every backpack. Not even one was blue with a brown bottom. I then checked all the 3rd grade backpacks. Not a one.

After stopping at three different stores on the way home and spending way more than I intended just to furnish this particular backpack, I was somewhat agitated at his request. As I shared the story with my husband that evening, I remarked how I just couldn't figure out why he wanted that specific backpack, blue with a brown bottom.

He looked at me with a strange look. "Cheryl, you have a blue backpack with a brown bottom."

The tears welled up inside me as they still do today. David got his blue backpack with the brown bottom. As it turns out, it was my last year teaching at the school. When I returned for a visit, David came running across the playground and hugged me. All the kids were hugging me, but in the whole year I had taught David, I could not even touch him. Just getting close would put him on edge.

The comments from the other kids also warmed my heart. "David is good now. He plays with us." Oh, how I had longed to hear those words. I had so wanted to help him attach and to let down his guard. Somehow, someway he had found his umbrella and braved the storm.

———

THIS STORY CIRCLED my head as we prepared for the start of the school year. During workshop week I had opportunities to think deeper about my students and teaching practices through two films. One film, *Most Likely to Succeed*,[2] pushed me to think about how students experience school and how learning could look and feel different. The students and teachers featured in this film built relationships and focused on learning with passion and a purpose.

The next film, *Paper Tigers*,[3] shared the story of high school students dealing with high levels of stress and trauma. It documented one school's success in understanding the effects of trauma and providing supportive relationships to facilitate healing and learning.

This learning, thinking, and reflecting swirled through my mind as I began my first interactions with the four boys in Mrs. G's class. I noticed the common theme of toxic stress and trauma could be transformed through building trust and creating new stories. Whether due to past experiences, unsettling home life, learning challenges or just the frustration of school required learning for which the student saw no immediate connection, these stories revealed the impact of stress on student learning. They also revealed the power of a teacher to pull these students out of the impending storm and into safety.

It also showed me the importance of grit. Angela Duckworth, a leading expert in this area, defines grit as "passion and perseverance for long term goals.[4]" Once again, while I saw it as something good for my students, I knew it was also essential for me. Day to day my job was challenging and hard. While some great memories stand out in my mind, there were many moments along the way where the only thing keeping me going was my ability to BE GRITTY.

PRACTICE - Be Gritty!

I have a necklace I put on every time I sit down to work on this story. It was given to me by a very special teacher. Thanks, Mrs. G. It's a raw pearl. It came with a card about grit. I hung the card on my bulletin board and read it every morning. The final line says, "she knows it's not what happens but how she chooses to respond, with perseverance in her mind and passion in her heart."[5] This is such a difficult thing to remember when you are in the middle of a storm.

HOW MUCH GRIT do you have? You can find out by taking Angela Duckworth's *Grit Scale*.[6] Duckworth developed the scale to measure grit and to assist in her research. She recommends using it mainly for self-reflection. It can help you think about how gritty you are. Of course, you probably have various levels of grit for different areas and projects in your life. For example, with this book I've been gritty. I've stuck with it for a few years learning to write. But my house-keeping, well, let's just say that's the kind of gritty you don't want. I probably need to focus less on my writing project and more on my cleaning.

Teachers, parents, and coaches need grit. Students and kids are long term projects, and they deserve the best of you. They also tend to take the most from you. In one of the staff bathrooms at my school we had a poster that read, *"The child that needs the most love will often ask for it in the most unloving of ways."* Sometimes when I am the brunt of these unloving solicitations for love and attention, it takes everything I have to keep being gritty.

That's why toxic stress is such a critical issue, not just for students but for teachers, parents, and coaches too. Stress by itself is not always a bad thing. You need some level of stress to be motivated to learn and do things. It's when this stress is compounded or relentless that it begins to take a major toll on health, thinking and coping skills. This is toxic stress.

———

STUDENTS EXPERIENCING trauma and toxic stress present many behaviors and learning problems in the classroom. Teachers, parents, and coaches can also suffer from dealing with this and from issues within their own families. Your past family history can also be a huge influence on the toxic stress and trauma you bring into your work.

Toxic stress is a critical issue for many students. Since I began writing this book it's become an even greater issue. The effects of the COVID-19 pandemic will have lasting implication on students, families, teachers, and communities. It has created toxic stress in probably every household. Therefore, toxic stress is an essential topic to understand. Parents, teachers and coaches need to recognize their own challenges with toxic stress and how to support students who suffer from it.

The teachers in the documentary *Paper Tiger* began changing their policies and practices after becoming familiar with the ACE (Adverse Childhood Experiences) study. The CDC-Kaiser Permanente ACE study from 1995 to 1997 was one of the first and largest studies to look at the effects of childhood stress on later health.[7] Over 17,000 participants completed confidential surveys regarding their childhood experiences and current health status. The results of this study, as well as much subsequent research, has shown that as the number of risk factors increases, so does the potential for developmental delays, emotional regulation, and health issues.

You can find much of the research related to this study, as well as the ACES questionnaire, on the ACES Too High Website.[8] Parents, teachers, and coaches can take this questionnaire themselves to understand their own risk factors. It is also a tool which can be used with students; however, it should be used in conjunction with a school counselor or social worker.

———

THE IMPLICATIONS of toxic stress on the developing brain are just beginning to be understood. The increased cortisol in the brain which triggers the child to flight, fight or freeze in response to negative stimuli becomes toxic if it cannot return to baseline levels.

Major childhood experiences such as the death of a parent, abuse and neglect have clearly shown negative effects on brain development. When children experience 6-7 risk factors, they have a 90-100% chance of developmental delays[9]. Stress impacts the development of the young brain and the ability of children to regulate behaviors. Many of the behavior and learning challenges confronting teachers, parents, and coaches, may be a direct result of toxic stress.

There are other sources of stress and its implications which are much less understood. Students who experience learning and behavior challenges are continuously confronted with highly stressful situations in the classroom. Bullying, taxing peer relationships and social media also produce stress responses which have yet to be researched and understood.

It's going to take a lot of grit to really create the necessary changes. Entire schools and education, as a whole, need to embrace these efforts. *Helping Traumatized Children Learn*[10] is an advocacy group working to do just that. Based on their work, they have developed five core ideas

- Traumatic experiences are prevalent in the lives of children.
- Traumatic experiences can impact learning, behavior, and relationships in school.
- Trauma sensitive schools help children feel safe to learn.
- Trauma sensitivity requires a whole-school effort.
- Helping traumatized children learn should be a major focus of education reform.

———

BEGIN your practice by learning about toxic stress and how it impacts the learning, behavior, and emotions of students. Develop trauma sensitive practices in your own classroom, home, or field, but don't stop there. Work with other teachers, parents, and school administrators to bring this issue to the forefront. Pay attention to the developing research and look for opportunities to advocate for and support students and adults suffering from the effects of toxic stress. Many non-profit groups also focus on this topic and may be interested in holding parent coffees, talks or meetings to support school efforts. Sometimes when the school environment isn't easy to change, there are other places where one can make a difference. **BE GRITTY!**

PURPOSE - Be Gritty!

BECAUSE OF 4 students my heart broke with their hurt and anger. I was stressed and anxious, but I had a strong support system, a whole tribe backing me up. My own ACES score was 0, which means I did not have any toxic stress factors. Over the years I had developed grit in many areas of my life. These four boys weren't as lucky. They had been failed many times by teachers, systems, even life itself. They could be gritty, but it wasn't always positive.

Grit is what gives you the power to keep going even when you feel knocked down. You need it and your students need it. Life rarely knocks us down without giving us an opportunity to rise up again. You have the power to create an extraordinary life for yourself and those around you. All it takes is a little faith and trust...oh and a little bit of pixie dust[11]...oops! I mean grit. :-) **BE GRITTY!**

BE GRITTY
step-by-step

4

Sometimes it's hard to recognize grit in the moment. Think about your stories. Play with memories you have about when you were gritty.

PLAY

Toxic stress impacts health, relationships and learning. Identify ways to mitigate stress for you or your students.

PRACTICE

Overcoming obstacles requires grit. Name 4 students and tell how you might be gritty for them. AND YOU!

PURPOSE

CREATE A BUCKET LIST

WHAT IS YOUR LEGACY? What do you want people to remember when they think about you? Create a bucket list of those things you want to accomplish or leave behind as your mark on the world.

TWELVE

GOOD-BYES

GOOD...BYE

How lucky I am to have something that makes saying goodbye so hard. -
Winnie the Pooh[1]

EACH OF THE boys handled the news and the inevitable end day in their own way. Each boy pulled and yanked at my heart.

Michael often sported the red and black of his namesake, Michael Jordan. His basketball shoes were well used as he darted around, mimicking plays. Michael was an active third grader. He rarely stood still or stopped talking.

After my announcement, there was a little less bounce in his step. Never at a loss for words, he continued to barrage me with questions about why I was moving and what a bad guy my husband must be for making me move. I could ignore his comments and pretend he still had his usual swagger, but the eyes were a different story. When he looked at me now, I couldn't help remembering our first meeting. I remembered his eyes as he challenged me.

"You won't take me. I'm stupid."

I remembered his eyes as his block tower grew and grew.

"Look at this you guys, I'm doing it!"

I remembered his eyes as we raced the Little Bits cars down the hallway.

"It's going. It's working. We did it!"

His eyes now held a question and an accusation at the same time.

"Why are you leaving us?!"

———

JERRY OFTEN HID his eyes behind a hood or a hat. The day he got a haircut, he pulled his hat way over his head even to the point of covering his eyes. Not only did he not want anyone to see, but he also didn't want to see them looking. Jerry was an expert at fleeing the scene as emotions boiled up inside him.

Jerry was like a balloon filled with air. I remember the first day we connected, and I saw the sparkle in his eyes.

"Guess what," he had smiled as I met him at his class. "I used to hate Mondays, but I like them now.

"Really? Why is that?"

"Because you come on Monday."

"That's enough to make you like Mondays?"

"That's enough to make me like everything."

But little by little, the air was slowly leaking out of the balloon. He didn't want one last day with me. He wanted to cut the string, float away, and get it over with as soon as possible.

I did what I could to ease the pain. On our last day, I gave each of the boys a rock with the word *scholar* on it and they decorated them.

I explained how I wanted them to know, even though I wouldn't be there, I would always believe in them, and I would try to stay connected. I tried to take a final photo and Jerry pulled his hat way over his eyes. All I could see was the monster on the hat he wore, not his eyes.

He ran from the classroom before our ending time. I found him in the hallway curled in a corner with his rock.

"I'm not."

I waited. "You're not what?"

"I'm not a scholar."

"Why?"

"Because I'm not smart."

"Whoever said scholars were smart? I told you they love to learn, and they work hard at it. You are a scholar. Look at me."

He kept his face down but looked up through the tops of his eyelids, anger and fear piercing my heart.

"I believe in you. I will keep believing in you until you can believe in yourself. You are a scholar. Keep the rock and don't forget."

———

AS ANGRY AS HE WAS, Larry could not hide his true personality. The same energy I noticed when he first walked into the cafeteria at breakfast and had marked him as a leader, continued to define and emanate from him. He carried with him a confidence and a charm. As tough as he acted though, he was a giver. He thrived on connection with others. I smiled thinking about how he had led his classmates in STEM activities.

"You can do it!"

"Let's work together guys!"

I remembered how he let grudges go in favor of keeping friendships intact.

"Are you ok? I know you had a rough go around with Rick"

"It's ok. He's still my man."

My heart probably would have died these last few weeks if it hadn't been for his generosity. Rather than avoid me or glare at me, he took every opportunity he could to connect with me. Over the next four weeks, every time I saw him in the hallway he came running over for a hug.

"You better write me."

"How long will you keep writing me?"

"As long as you keep writing me back, I will keep writing you. I had a third grader once that is in his 20's now and he still sends me a Christmas card every year. I still talk with my kindergarten teacher. We can write as long as you want, Larry."

"Ok, I'm going to keep writing you, even in high school."

"Even in college," I added plugging it as an option one more time.

"Yeah," he answered, not yet convinced.

———

MY HUSBAND ALWAYS SAYS, "Nothing worth having comes easy." Rick didn't come easy, and he wasn't about to go down easy either. He could sell sawdust to a lumber mill. He had frequently used his power of persuasion on me.

"Please, can we have lunch today?"

"We'll help you clean up."

"Your son will understand if you are late to his concert."

"How much time do you need to get to your meeting? You can meet with us and then go to your meeting."

He was a charmer and I often fell prey to his eyes and words.

"You know Miss W. is never going to be as good as you."

"You can just tell your husband you're not going to move."

"Don't you want to stay here?"

He worked hard over the next few weeks to get as many moments as he could. He never once passed up an opportunity for lunch or a hug. But all the energy spent sparing me his hurt had to go somewhere

"Well, it's official." Mrs. G said as we met for lunch. "Rick won't be going to the track and field day."

"What? That's his thing. He was looking forward to it."

"I know, but he got into another fight at recess. The last few days have been bad. It just really feels like there needs to be some consequences."

"I guess. He's just losing so much. I knew this was going to be hard."

"Yeah. It is."

———

IT WAS HARD. Because of four and so much more. My other students wanted me to stay. My colleagues wanted me to stay. My kids wanted to stay. I wanted to stay. Sometimes life sends you in a different direction than you plan. Deep in my heart, I knew there was a reason. I hoped I wasn't just another person who left, but a person who had changed the direction of their path. I hoped I left them with enough.

PLAY - Good...Bye

In teaching and parenting, like most people, I wanted to control the outcome. I sought out the perfect plan, no surprises, and the certainty of the outcomes I desire. I fought against every curve ball life sent my way, believing it was somehow trying to get me. But this time was different.

My husband losing his job, having to move from a home and friends we loved, and confronting financial challenges were just some of the personal realities pulling at me. Professionally, I had finally moved into a leadership position in the district and had the job and opportunities I desired.

It felt in many ways as if life was happening to me. But for some reason, as I battled against the life changes confronting me, I changed my usual tactics. Rather than playing defense and shutting down, I became more vulnerable and opened up.

———

CHALLENGES IN LIFE have a way of surfacing our vulnerabilities. You realize just how vulnerable you are when confronting illness, job loss or the death of a loved one. Most of us shy away from situations where we feel vulnerable. We tend to numb vulnerability with perfectionism and maybe even addiction. Many of the behavior problems I notice in students and the boys in this story are defense mechanisms created to protect themselves from feeling vulnerable.

According to shame researcher, Brené Brown, the people who have the strongest sense of belonging and wholeheartedness embrace vulnerability.[2] They embrace the fact that there are no guarantees. They invest in relationships regardless of what they might get from them. They invest in outcomes they can't control or predict.

Being vulnerable requires courage, compassion, and connection. Courage in this sense is the ability to tell the story of who you are with your whole heart. Compassion is the ability to be kind to yourself first and then extend that kindness to those around you. Connection results from these first two acts and is a result of being authentic. It comes from being able to be who you are to yourself and others.

As I look back, I see how life was not just happening for me but through me. It pushed me into a space where I could choose to be vulnerable. When I did so at the right place and right time, it allowed a safe space for the boys to be vulnerable.

———

BRENÉ BROWN'S research on shame and vulnerability captures what happened here. But it is still missing part of the picture. Vulnerability was a key factor in my being able to open up to the boys. It was also a contributing factor in them laying down their defenses. But it was more than just putting myself out there that spurred such a connection. Besides being vulnerable, I was urgent.

It's something I always feel in teaching. For me there are always two sides of the coin. On the one side, there is never enough time to do everything or cover everything. On the other, there is always tomorrow, or next week or even next year. My feelings in this case could only be described as urgent optimism.

From the beginning I knew our time together was limited, even more so than in a regular school year. I knew I would be disrupting the normal patterns and transitions of departing and saying good-bye. This knowledge made me acutely aware of the need to do as much as I could to lay the foundation for my departure. In many ways, I felt as if I was establishing my legacy and I invested as much as I could into making my last moments count.

———

AS I MET with the four boys and each of my classes for the last time, I shared with each of them some of my favorite things about them as we reflected on the learning we did together. Each of my students were given a rock with the word *scholar* carefully printed on it. Most of my students had begun to internalize what this word meant, but I felt compelled to leave them with a lasting token of the commitment they had made to love learning and work hard.

I didn't realize it until later, but these moments were my last lecture. The last lecture is an academic tradition where a faculty member who is leaving is given a last opportunity to lecture to the student body. In September 2007, Randy Pausch, gave his last lecture, *The Last Lecture: Really Achieving Your Childhood Dreams*.[3] After being diagnosed with terminal cancer, Randy used his last days to inspire his children and the world to pursue their dreams. Rather than lamenting the fact that there wasn't enough time, Randy used every moment he had left to share his message of inspiration and hope.

This lecture, which was later turned into a book, was shared with me shortly after I had my last moments at my school and with the four boys. I instantly connected with how Randy wanted to use his last moments to deliver a message of hope and to make things ok for those he was leaving behind. He made it a GOOD...BYE.

PRACTICE - Good...Bye

Recently my grandmother celebrated her 100th birthday. It was her lifelong goal to celebrate her 100th birthday. Shortly after, she passed away peacefully, with no pain or suffering. What many don't know is that over forty years ago she was given only 3 years to live. She decided the only way to beat that fate was to live a life full of positivity. Following her funeral our family heard countless stories of the inspiration she had been to others. When we laid her to rest it wasn't just a funeral it was more of a celebration of a life well lived. It was a *good-bye*.

CREATING the life you want can take a bit of effort. My grandmother did it by reading her Bible and just about every book on positive thinking she could find. Until the last few years of her life, she continued to write book reports on every book she read. She wrote positive quotes and constantly shared positive messages.

I always admired her discipline and commitment to self-development. It's something that doesn't come easily to me. I can sometimes be a bit of a glass is half-empty kind of person. When I said good-bye and we moved I wasn't exactly happy about my new life. It wasn't exactly following the trajectory I had planned.

Without a job yet, I found myself moping around a bit. Finally, I decided enough was enough and I better get busy with living. I decided if I was going to be a writer I had better start writing and reading. I decided to take a page from my grandma's book and look for some positive thinking books. I stumbled across a book called, *The Miracle Morning* by Hal Elrod.[4] I figured my mornings could probably use a miracle, so I downloaded it and began reading.

————

I IMMEDIATELY LOVED Hal's story. After a near death experience, he developed a routine to make the most of his mornings and set the tone for his entire day. The next part I wasn't so happy about. Basically, he encouraged getting up every morning and following a whole routine designed to give you the best start to your day and to foster personal development.

I fought the idea of getting up any earlier, but the more I read I was intrigued. Finally, I decided to try it. I had a great morning. Then another and another. Before long it became a ritual. I kept the habit consistently for over a year. Since then, I've had moments when I fell off the Miracle Morning wagon and I've tweaked it a bit to fit me better, but I will admit there is something to starting your morning on a positive note.

This book has been so widely embraced there are now extension books like Miracle Morning for Writers, Families, Couples and yes, even a Miracle Morning for Teachers. Hal tried the Miracle Morning out with teachers and schools and the results were amazing. Students had more energy and focus and were really excited about the morning routine.

I don't want to give too much of the book away as it's really a good read and I won't do it justice in a summary, but one of the key ideas is to have a vision for your life and affirmations to support that vision. One of the things I discovered through this story is sometimes when you start with the vision of what you want your life or impact to be at the end, when you say good-bye, what you really want becomes very clear.

This clarity becomes the driving force. How to get there and the stumbling blocks along the way are easier to navigate with a clear idea of where you are going. It's also helpful to commit these goals to paper and continue to refresh your memory with them. Writing a daily journal or reflection can be a way to capture a future hope and dream to share with yourself and reflect on later. A fun electronic version of this is Future Me.[5] Using this service, you can create an e-mail to yourself which will be sent on a specific date you indicate.

The main thing is to make yourself, and creating a life well-lived, a priority. The best legacy we can leave is a life we loved and to have enjoyed it to its fullest. Live a full life. Make it a **GOOD-BYE.**

PURPOSE - Good...Bye

BECAUSE OF 4 students, we said goodbye and grieved in different ways. When something is lost, you grieve. While it goes through typical stages, it looks different for everyone. Sometimes the best you can do is allow space for those emotions to surface and provide the grace needed to work through it.

In Minnesota, there is a joke about the Minnesota goodbye. Because so much time is spent waiting for cars to warm up, the farewell at the door often lags on and on. But all things must come to end. Some endings seem to come too soon, and some don't seem to come soon enough. You don't always get the ending you want, but you have a far greater chance of making it a good one if you greet each day as a miracle and move through it with urgent optimism. Make your moment count. If you've given it your best, saying farewell will be hard but worth it. Make it a **GOOD-BYE.**

GOOD - BYE
step-by-step

Endings are often the first step to new beginnings.
Play with ideas you have for making your last moments count.

PLAY

Saying good-bye is easier when you know you have fully lived the experience. Identify things you can do to embrace life.

PRACTICE

Make your moment count. Name 4 students and tell how you might intentionally show up for them. AND YOU!

PURPOSE

CREATE A DOG TAG

WHAT WORDS DO you want put into the world? What do you want to leave behind to make a difference in someone else's life? Create a dog tag to capture words of inspiration for you or for your child, student or player.

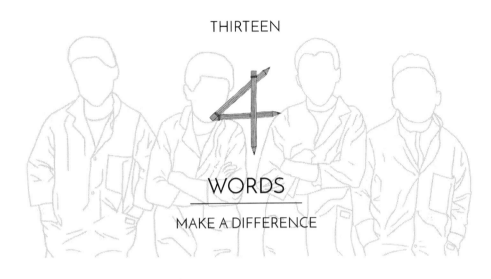

THIRTEEN

4

WORDS

MAKE A DIFFERENCE

The willingness to show up changes us. It makes us a little braver each time. -Brené Brown[1]

IT HAD BEEN a long day. I watched my son, Ben, turn and head up to bed. Suddenly, it was as if the life had been suckcd out of him. He collapsed to the floor just as I swept him onto my lap. His body lay limp in my arms as he whimpered.

"I can't do it mom! I just can't!"

"Shhh" I murmured rocking him back and forth. Eleven was way too big to be held on his mother's lap, but at that moment he felt as small as he had when he was first placed in my arms. My instincts kicked in and I simply sat rocking him gently, letting him experience his grief and helping him continue to breath.

In and out I breathed. Slowly he began to mimic my breath. His body relaxed as he gave into his emotions. Sobs turned to whimpers and then sniffles.

Somehow, I remained strong. Maybe it was the mother's instinct to put myself aside for my child. Perhaps I had no tears left for myself. It had only been a day since I had said my goodbyes. I didn't have much water left for tears after that.

———

I HAD STOPPED by the school-wide Jump Rope for Heart assembly to spend a few last minutes with my four boys. Almost as if I were a magnet and they were heavy metal, they emerged through the crowd and hung at my side. We cheered as their teacher stepped into an icy, cold tank as part of the reward challenge. I anxiously watched the clock with the rest of the teachers wondering how we were going to conclude this assembly and get all the kiddos organized in time for buses.

Just as it seemed to be over, our crazy 1st grade teachers jumped up. "We just wanted to remind everyone today is Dr. Peterson's last day. You might want to send her off with a hug or a high five on your way out."

I felt the light touch of Mrs. G behind me, holding me up, preparing me for what she knew would come and I was only just beginning to understand. From behind I could feel Rick's arms in a bear hug with his head buried against my back. Around me were swarms of students reaching in for a hug. Some hugged quickly and moved on. Others held on for dear life, alligator tears streaming down their faces.

———

IT TOOK a few promises of a final goodbye to calm Rick as he was beginning to push away students coming in for a hug. I managed to persuade him to head down to his class for his coat with the promise I would meet him there.

Slowly the swarm retreated, and I walked a few stragglers back to class. I kept reassuring them I would write and connect with them electronically. Some students I had known several years. We'd been working up to the goodbye for a few weeks. Others, I only knew from brief stops in their classroom, yet many of them shed tears too.

———

I MADE one last stop by Mrs. G's room to say goodbye. Jerry gave a quick hug and moved on. Larry, not able to say goodbye again, moved to the back of the room. Rick employed full use of his persuasive skills.

"Me and Michael can wait for the bus in your room, right?"

"Let's go right now. You don't need to say goodbye to anyone else."

"Come on, Dr. Peterson."

We waited for the buses; the two boys trying to throw footballs and generally cause chaos and me trying to prepare for our final goodbye.

"Bus 39" came across the loudspeaker.

"That's me. See ya." Michael sprinted off with a quick hug.

I tried to keep the conversation light with Rick. "So, you know I'll be in Chicago. That's where the Bears play. I might even get to see a game."

Rick shrugged. Every minute seemed like an eternity, but went too fast at the same time. Finally, Rick's bus was called.

He grabbed me around the waist and buried his head, no longer able to hold back his tears but not wanting to show me. I could feel the connection we had stretching, not wanting to let go, but knowing it could only stretch so far.

"You can do this," I whispered, and we began to walk. "I won't just leave," I promised, "I will write and we will find ways to stay in touch. I believe in you and you can do this!"

The walk to the bus felt like a walk down death row. The end was too soon. We had only just begun. I only hoped it was enough. At the last moment, I peeled his arms away and pushed him off. He went to the bus; I smiled bravely, turned, and cried.

———

I KNEW what Ben was feeling at that moment. I knew how it felt as if everything he loved was going to be gone. I knew the moving date, once so far away, was upon us. I knew he needed my strength. Suddenly, I jumped up and ran to my bag. I knew this was the moment. Throughout the week I had been giving my students rocks with the words *scholar* printed on them. I saw how having something tangible to hang on to helped. As I pulled Ben back into my lap, I handed him a small box.

"I can't," he pleaded again.

I opened the box, took out the dog tag, and slowly slipped it over his neck. "You can," I encouraged him, reading the words as I caught his eyes. "You are braver than you believe, stronger than you seem, smarter than you think, and loved more than you'll ever know."

"I can't," he whispered a little less forcefully.

"You are brave, strong, smart and loved. These four words are all you need to tell yourself right now. You don't have to do everything; you just have to do one thing at a time. Right now, just say the words. Later, you can believe them. Brave. Strong. Smart. Loved."

PLAY - Make a Difference

Love. It's not a word we use very often in teaching. There are many good reasons for teachers to be careful about how they interact with students. The newspaper holds plenty of stories of molestation and abuse. Teachers need to be vigilant in understanding this issue and how behaviors they exhibit may make it easier for predators to take advantage of children. This is a serious issue and should not be taken lightly. But taking advantage of a child in a physical or emotional way is abuse, not love.

———

LOVE IS something different and it's something we are lacking in our classrooms, relationships, and society. Love is an extremely powerful emotion. It's difficult to describe and define. Most often it is better captured through poetry and prose. It is a powerful emotion. 1 Corinthians 13:4.7-8 describes love as patient and kind, always protecting and trusting. Love hopes, perseveres, and never fails.[2]

When you look at a person with love in your heart and in your eyes, it makes a difference. It affects how you look and respond to the person, as well as how they respond to you. Sometimes this is not an easy emotion to cultivate. There are times when our own histories and past experiences get in the way. While we may want to love all our students, quite frequently we don't. When a child is difficult, or has difficulties, it may be hard to love the child.

———

THE TEDDY STALLARD story,[3] is a perfect example of this. Like many of us do, Teddy's teacher initially judged him on the picture he presented of himself. Teddy was messy and uninterested in school. He did not have friends and was apathetic toward his school-work. Teddy didn't want to learn. So, what was a teacher to do? It wasn't until Teddy's teacher read his past files and realized Teddy had once been an energetic, bright boy until his mother died of a terminal illness.

In the two years prior to entering her classroom, Teddy had experienced a steady decline in support and in his own attitude and motivation to school. Teddy's teacher made a conscious decision to love Teddy. Not only did Teddy turn around and develop a lasting relationship with his teacher, but she also changed in more ways than she ever imagined. She learned to teach children, not subjects. This is the power of love. Love changes both the giver and the receiver.

———

I CAN'T THINK of a more powerful example of this in action than the documentary film, *Love Them First: Lessons from Lucy Lane Elementary*.[4] This documentary tells a powerful story of how a principal created a school and culture where the most important thing is to love students first. This story captures the difficulties and struggles with behavior and academic challenges. It shows how stress and trauma impact the lives of the teachers, families, and students. It also shows how time and time again, love overcomes. **MAKE A DIFFERENCE** by letting every child know they are brave, strong, smart, and loved.

PRACTICE - Make a Difference

A common theme throughout this book is to commit to your practice before teaching or using it with others. Love is no exception. It is impossible to love others if you do not first love and care for yourself. However, this is something we often forget and think we can bypass. Parents, teachers, and coaches often put the needs of the children before themselves. This works for a period of time but tends to result in resentment and anger. Often it is acting out of obligation rather than love.

———

THINK about the directions given by the flight attendants as they review the safety procedures. "Put your own facemask on first." In love, your words are the facemask. The words you chose will either give you the life force you need or drain you of all your energy. Think about the words you say to yourself. Would you say them to a friend? Would you say them to a child? How are you using your words to love yourself?

One way to begin paying attention to your self-talk and turning around negative messages is to find a picture of yourself as a child. When you find yourself engaging in negative self-talk, try to say those words out loud to that child. Most people will find that difficult to do. Then look at that child with love in your heart. What do you want to say to that child? How can you extend your love to that child? Now extend that same love to the grown-up version of yourself.

Another way to improve your self-talk can be as simple as practicing it when you drink your morning coffee. In her book, *Coffee Self-Talk*,[5] Kristin Helmstetter shares a process for creating positive affirmations and a regular practice of cultivating positive self-talk over your morning coffee.

———

IN CHAPTER 4, meditation was presented as a technique for reducing stress and getting in tune with the present. Meditation can also be a useful technique for cultivating love. In a loving kindness meditation, you focus on positive thoughts and extending that message to others. The *Greater Good in Action* website[6] provides a detailed description of this practice as well as a script for guiding your meditation.

As you are cultivating love for yourself, you can also work on extending this love to others. Let's face it, some people are difficult to love. But love isn't just some magic that happens, you can choose love. Sometimes when you work with a colleague or your student, the first thought is not one of love. It may be judgement based on their appearance, frustration caused by past experiences, or even fear of their anger and resentment.

You have the power to change your words and reactions. You have the choice to offer love. As you approach the person, say silently to yourself, "I love you." As you do this, your eyes and your body language will convey a different message. It may not be received or reciprocated at first, but over time love can have tremendous power.

While I have had many of my own examples of this, the Chen Miller Story[7] captures the essence of the power teachers have to offer love to a child who is asking for it in a challenging way. In this story, Chen Miller talks about a little boy who spit and cursed, and yet she told him he had a big heart and she spoke to him with love in her heart and eyes. After several times of doing this, he eventually chose her as his teacher. Chen Miller later reveals she was once that child herself and all but one teacher had given up on her. The love of a teacher is what turned things around for her.

———

HOW DO you become someone who makes a difference? Be more. Use the stories and resources in this book to improve yourself and your ability to uncover potential in young people and in yourself.

Parents can often improve communication with teachers by approaching them first with love. I often find if I share information about my childrens' learning challenges with teachers at the beginning of the year in a positive way, it helps them get to know them as more than a student, but as a person.

Teachers, take the time to get to know each student. Really care about who they are as a person, not just how they do in your class. Find out what they need. There are many ways to do this. You can greet each student at the door as they arrive to your class and notice them. What emotional state are they in? What is going on with them? Use interest surveys and focus groups to find out what is important to your students and what they need. If a student is struggling, don't assume they don't care or don't want to do better. This is most often a defense mechanism.

Find any small glimmer in a student and continue to encourage it to grow. Have a slogan or phrase you believe and can convey even if you struggle to find something good in a child. Use the words of Chen Miller, "you have a big heart; you are good." Or MAKE A DIFFERENCE by using the words of Winnie the Pooh, "You are braver than you believe, stronger than you seem, smarter than you think, and loved more than you'll ever know."[8]

PURPOSE - Make a Difference

BECAUSE OF 4 students I loved and let go. Four words gave me the strength to face my sadness and comfort my son: brave, strong, smart, and LOVED. We all have so much capacity to be more. Sometimes it just takes digging down deep and remembering who we are and what we have within us.

Give and receive love. Don't wait for someone else to make a difference for a child. Be more! Be the teacher, parent or coach who can **MAKE A DIFFERENCE**. I know you can because,

---

"You are **braver** than you believe,

stronger than you seem,

smarter than you think,

and **loved** more than you'll ever know."

-A.A. Milne[9]

MAKE A DIFFERENCE
step-by-step

Words are powerful. Play with ideas you have for using words to inspire yourself and others.

PLAY

Self-talk impacts your abilities.
Identify strategies you can use to improve your self-talk.

PRACTICE

The words you use make a difference. Name 4 students and identify how words can make a difference for them. >AND YOU!

PURPOSE

FOURTEEN

PROMISES

TELL YOUR STORY

Every new beginning comes from some other beginning's end. -
Semisonic[1]

LEAVING WAS like finishing a good book. The story left me with mixed emotions. I was so sad to see it end, but exhilarated. I had made a difference. But what now? Would the four boys continue to see themselves as scholars? Would they feel as if one more adult just abandoned them? I was passionate about what I was doing and wanted to see it through, but I was also moving seven hours away. My own kids were starting a new middle school. It certainly was not an ideal time to pull them from their social groups and a place they called home.

But a promise is a promise. I promised not to just leave. As I drove out of town, I dropped off letters for every one of my students. Each one was personalized, mentioning something I appreciated about them. For the teacher taking over my groups, I left a package with a note.

"Thanks for taking such good care of these students. I know they will grow to love you. Here is a fun game to help you get to know them and ease the transition. I also left an envelope with a note for each group. Focus on building your relationships, and all will go well. I'm so happy you were selected for this position. You are the perfect person to help these kids through the end of the year."

A few weeks later, Mrs. G received a package from me. In it were 4 dog tags with the words, "Always remember, you are braver than you believe, stronger than you seem, smarter than you think and loved more than you know." She took a moment with each of the boys and gave them the gift. Each of them held on to it firmly, pushed back tears and put it in a secure place.

MY FIRST VISIT back was only a few weeks after I left. My son's hockey association had an academic award ceremony. I had promised if he got the grades to qualify, we would come back. This was one promise I had to keep. He worked hard despite some challenges and the emotional rollercoaster of a year. His outgoing personality and charm had served him well in elementary school. In elementary school, having dyslexia was only a minor inconvenience since he was able to learn easily and retain information shared orally.

Suddenly, in middle school, the rules changed and information had to be read. In his STEM elementary school, the students actively engaged in learning with hands-on projects, experiential learning, and discussions. He thrived, learning content by Skyping with experts or participating in collaborative projects where he was encouraged to work with a group. While we knew reading issues existed and worked with tutors to develop his skills, it did not seem to impact his learning.

In middle school, his opportunities for conversation were limited to the two-minute passing period. He was encouraged to talk less, listen less and somehow learn more. Even math became a challenge as more and more words replaced numbers. He earned a trip back to Minnesota for this award.

———

I COULDN'T COME BACK without stopping in to visit the boys. Larry, Jerry, and Michael met with me for a small group. We played a game and chatted. I introduced a new game and explained they might not want to make a mistake when they wrote their clue.

"Of course, we can make a mistake," said Larry without missing a beat. "We're scholars now and scholars make mistakes. It's how we learn."

I smiled. I knew I did something right. I showed them pictures of my new home and shared with them pictures of me with my new chickens.

"You have chickens?"

"Weird!"

"What do they eat?"

———

BUT OUR CONVERSATION WAS STRAINED. I wondered if perhaps it was better to just say goodbye and be done. School years end, people get new jobs, leaving happens. This felt like slowly pulling back the Band-Aid on a fresh wound. Maybe it was better to just rip it off and be done. But it was more than just the awkwardness of saying hello and goodbye again. Rick was missing. My heart ached for him. I knew he would be upset to miss my visit. I was upset to miss him. I wondered how things fell apart so quickly. How could a third grader get expelled? I knew the school did not have much of a choice. He lost control at recess and the safety of other students and teachers was at stake. What if I was there? Would the outcome have been any different?

———

GOING BACK HOME or visiting with old friends always seems too long and too short at the same time. The physical distance created when you live far away from someone separates you from them. Anyone who has ever sustained a long-distance relationship understands this drill. While distance makes the heart grow fonder, it also makes it awkward. You spend the first part of your time together catching up on what has happened and the last part preparing to leave again.

While you want to make the most of every minute, you also don't want to get too close again because you know the leaving part is inevitable and it hurts. Jerry seemed to have the keenest sense of this. You could almost see the invisible shield around him, protecting him. He didn't look at me. He was short with the other boys.

"You're not playing right. You always take over."

"When can we go back to class?"

I wanted to cry. Only a few months ago Jerry was telling me how he liked Mondays because he got to see me. Today I was as welcome as a trip to the dentist for a filling. I tried to make the parting easier this time. We already said our goodbyes. I tried to push it off as just a see you next time.

Again, I left notes for every one of my students. I also picked up a pile of notes many had left for me. I left each of the boys a note for their parents. Despite multiple attempts, I still had not made direct contact with any of the parents. I wanted them to know how proud I was of the boys and what a difference they made to me.

———

PROMISES

THE CAR RIDE back was longer than usual. A promise was kept, but it left us feeling a little hollow. We realized as much as we didn't feel at home in our new place, this was no longer home either.

My daughter suddenly broke the silence with a strange request. "Can we go back for the last day of school at our old school? We could get our yearbook and get it signed and stuff. It would be like our last goodbye."

"Yeah, I'll see what we can do," I responded, not quite promising. Part of me jumped at the chance to go again. Missing Rick bothered me and I didn't want to end the year without one last connection. But my concern immediately turned to my daughter. The move had been particularly difficult on her. Not one to make friends easily, she held tight to her old friends. Most of her time was spent talking to them on the phone or using video chats.

Always a bundle of creativity and energy in the summers, school seemed to damper more and more of her personality. Her creativity served her well in many of the experiential learning opportunities but punished her on multiple choice tests. Writing for her became a creative outlet and escape, but lost much of its draw as teachers placed more and more expectations on how it should be done.

A naturally keen observer, she picked up all kinds of details in class but struggled with taking a note that would help her connect to the learning. If she did manage to copiously take down all the verbiage thrown at her, she often had little to no understanding of what it was she was supposed to learn. Increasingly demoralized, her attitude toward school became lackadaisical. Now without a social group to dull the tedium of her day, she was suffering.

———

I MADE heroic efforts to make this almost-promise a reality. I talked to all the school personnel I could. I called old teachers and counselors. I was hoping for anyone to bend the rules just a little bit to help her have some closure. I wanted her to have a signed 8th grade yearbook. To most people I suppose these little social, emotional things seem like nothing, but I have seen how connection and relationships are everything.

We finished our school year in Illinois a week before Minnesota, so we loaded up the car and made the trek again. I was still working on trying to make good on my promise. I got my final response as I checked my e-mail from the hotel that evening. "We are sorry, but the last day is a rather hectic day at school. We will be taking finals and there will be no yearbook signing. Elena's yearbook can be picked up at the office."

"Ok," was the only response I got when I shared the news, but the disappointment in her eyes told the whole story. My heart broke again.

"We can have Alex get it for you and pick her up from school. You can celebrate the last day together. Maybe she can get a few people to sign it."

"Yeah."

———

WE SPENT the morning visiting my old school. I met with the four boys for one last time. It was the last day of school, so they were a bit hyped up. My visit was just another goodbye for the day.

"Who's she?" asked Michael with the same attitude he had first greeted me with some many months before. Now that I had been raising chickens, I had a new understanding for what it meant to "rustle feathers." Michael was trying to establish the pecking order.

My daughter, a bit of a moody teen, and not happy she was spending her day at my old school replied, "I'm her daughter," and then turning to me said, "Are they always this rude?"

"Hey, you're the one that's rude."

"You don't even know me."

"Yeah, you don't know me either," Michael retorted.

"Ok, guys," I stepped in before it got any uglier. I glared at my daughter with my best don't you dare say another word look and engaged the boys in a game. We talked about their summer plans and I encouraged them to write to me over the summer. We took some final pictures together and parted.

———

I GOT to spend the day yearbook signing and saying farewell to lots of kids. It was the closure I and many of them needed. Saying goodbye in March just didn't seem right. Somehow the last day of school makes goodbyes easier. There's an energy and excitement to it. Just around the corner is summer and the hopes of a new year.

Fortunately, a beautiful day paved our entrance into summer. I was able to run and play with my students on the playground as they shared with me their summer plans and hopes for next year. The last day of school for me is always a lot like New Year's Eve. While it's sad to say goodbye to the year past, there is so much energy and excitement about what's ahead.

This time as Rick and I made the final trek to the bus, it wasn't as much a goodbye. I had kept my promise. I hadn't just left. I told him I would always think about him and hope for him. He could reach out to me whenever he wanted. We both smiled and waved goodbye.

———

I KEPT MY PROMISE. A few months later, on the first day of school, Jerry, Rick, and Larry found a letter from me on their desk. Michael had moved with no forwarding information. I told each of the boys about their new teachers and how they were expecting them to be scholars. I had also written to the teachers and told them how important relationship was to these boys and what they were capable of doing when someone believed in them.

I continued to send notes throughout the year. Jerry wrote back several times. Each time his writing ability improved, and I could almost see him growing and learning as his letters got better and better.

Rick and Larry didn't write, but when I stopped in for a short visit, they still had their smiles and spirit. They were proud of how their reading was improving. Rick showed me the new math he was learning. He also continued to develop his negotiation skills, working it so that he could have a few extra minutes with me. They were happy to see me, but they had moved on and grown up. Just as it should be.

————

AS TEACHERS, we only have students for a short time and then pass them on to the next teacher, grade, or life opportunity. We hope the next teacher will love them as we have and discover their gifts and talents. For those we haven't reached yet, we hope the next teacher will be able to uncover what remained hidden for us. We know the end of the year really isn't an end at all. It's just the beginning.

PLAY - Tell Your Story

Sometimes I can't sleep at night. I see the faces of my students and my children. I wonder what will happen next. Will the next teacher see the leadership skills in the boys, or will they see trouble? Will my own kids find teachers who love them and see their potential, or will they be forced to continue playing a school game they will never win?

Over the years I've had countless students I worried over and wondered what might happen. I've worried about my own chil-drens' struggles and challenges and my fight with a system that just doesn't seem to understand the whole is more than the sum of the parts. I used to feel hopeless and share the same sentiment I've heard from several teachers. You can try, but you can't change the system. For years, that is what I believed. I worked within the system and did my best despite it.

Because of four, I realize my best was not nearly good enough. Despite pockets of success, if you really measured what matters, I have collected far more failures than trophies. Before I was ok with that. I got good feedback from parents. My performance reviews were positive. Most of my students experience academic growth. But these measures no longer matter to me.

I don't care if kids are college ready, pass their standardized tests, or can check off any number of learning standards. Because of 4, I have a new set of criteria for evaluating my progress. I have a formula for learning.

PLAY + PRACTICE + PURPOSE

I ALSO HAVE a set of guiding principles:

- Lean in
- Believe in miracles
- Inspire a thirst for learning and scholarly habits
- Be in the moment
- Scholars love learning and work hard
- It's playtime!
- Grow your ideas
- Leap and Lead
- Dream big, start small, act now
- Build a firm foundation
- Be gritty
- Live the life of your dreams and make it a good-bye
- I can make a difference because I am brave, strong, smart, and loved

- Tell the story **Because of 4** and...Be MORE!

———

YOU CAN'T OFTEN CHANGE a system, but you can rewrite the story. At the beginning of the school year, the movie, *Most Likely to Succeed*,[2] inspired me to think differently about my students. In screening this movie around the country, Ted Dintersmith, set out to change education. Instead, he discovered a growing number of disrupters changing the face of education one classroom, one district, one state at a time. In his book, *What Schools Could Be*,[3] Dintersmith paints a picture of courageous teachers inspiring and engaging students with meaningful learning experiences.

These teachers and leaders are seeing the same things I saw because of four students. Parents all over the country who were suddenly forced into more of a teaching role in the last few years have also begun to see these things. They have raised their voices at school board meetings and sometimes taken on the challenge of home-schooling. Whether you school at home, coach on a field or teach in a classroom, we all have a responsibility to find ways to bring back the joy of learning, to build solid foundations and work together as communities.

Students should be the focus of education, not scores, not content, not curriculum. These things matter, but in balance, not a pendulum swing. When we begin to see what each student can do and needs to do to continue to grow rather than measuring what all students know on a specified set of outcomes, I believe we will be way closer to getting things right.

Across the country, a growing number of teachers and parents are disrupting the system. They are doing whatever it takes to get it right for their student, their school, their community. They are daring bravely, making mistakes, and believing in their students. They aren't following the next shiny red ball but looking closely at the problems and challenges facing them and creating opportunities.

Because of 4, I do too. This is my story. Now it's your turn. **TELL YOUR STORY.**

PRACTICE - Tell Your Story

As this story began, Dr. Manny Scott[4] kicked off the school year as our guest speaker. He was one of the writers portrayed in the film, *Freedom Writers*.[5] In this film, a teacher transforms a classroom of high school students by believing in them, building relationships, and giving their stories a voice. It's a powerful story and illustrates how one teacher can make a difference.

Dr. Manny Scott shares his story with teachers around the world telling how one teacher turned him from failing and dropping out to earning a doctorate degree. He now uses his talents in speaking to work with students and teachers to inspire them to overcome these stressors and change the trajectory of their lives. Scott shares how writing his story helped reframe his life and shares how you can do the same.

As I went to cite the reference for Dr. Manny Scott, I found it particularly interesting how his name came up on the citation. *Scholar.* Dr. Manny Scott once saw himself as a gangster. Today he sees himself as a scholar. Dr. Manny Scott's tagline says it all, "Even on your worst day, you can be a student's best hope."[6]

———

STUDENTS NEED HOPE. To extend hope to a student, you need to understand their world from their perspective. Too often teachers, parents, and coaches are caught in their own worlds and lack the empathy needed to support young people. In education, decisions about what happens in classrooms are often made on the political floor rather than on the floors of schools. Too often the end users, the students, have no voice in the system.

Shadow a Student Challenge[7] is a movement to change this and give educators and leaders insight into the lives of the students they serve.

Dintersmith[8] highlights this movement in his book, *What Schools Could Be*, and shares the story of a school district in Cedar Rapids, IA. This school created innovative changes based on the shadow a student experience. One of the powerful components of this movement is a step-by-step guide to implementing your own shadow experience.

The resources on the website clearly identify the steps to the process. It also provides support resources for planning a shadow experience and shares incredible stories of how educators made small improvements based on what they define as hacks. These hacks are small, well-planned initiatives leaders can take to impact change based on the insight gained from their shadow experience.

———

MANY FAILED educational reforms have tried to take on the whole system and change everything based on a new concept, curriculum, or content. The *Shadow a Student* movement shifts the focus from the solution to the student and the unique problem or challenges facing the student. The changes are not large scale, but small and usually impactful.

My own experience because of four students illustrates the power of such a model. Perhaps I haven't impacted a whole system, yet. But small changes with four students continue to lead to bigger and bigger changes with other teachers, the school, and the district. In sharing my learning with other leaders in other schools, I also began to see my story creating a ripple effect in other districts as well.

You may never see the full impact of the ripple you create, but if you never take that step, there will never be a wave. My journey began because of four students. I'm inspired to continue because I see them everywhere. I see them in the news stories on tv. I wonder if they will make it and stand on the stage someday like Dr. Scott or if their life will end too soon, never being fully lived.

When I want to give up and quit I can't because I know they are out there somewhere. Maybe they are in your classroom or on your playing field or friends with your child. Do you see what they can do? Do you see what you can do because of four? **TELL YOUR STORY.**

PURPOSE - Tell Your Story

BECAUSE OF 4 students, I have a story to tell. It's a story of growth, challenge and staying in the moment. It's all my experiences, learning and ideas woven together. It's sharing my heart and my mind. Living this story gave me hope and that's what I wanted to share with you.

———

BECAUSE OF 4 I hope you are inspired and encouraged to **LEAN IN** and create your own moments. I hope you **BELIEVE IN MIRACLES** and help every child know they are truly a miracle by letting your face light up. I hope you inspire a **THIRST FOR LEARNING** and scholarly habits. I hope you take time for mindfulness so you can **BE IN THE MOMENT**. I hope you discover **WHAT'S YOUR WORD** to keep you going or inspire you. When **IT'S PLAYTIME**, I hope you play and grow your idea so it can **CHANGE THE WORLD**. I hope you **LEAP AND LEAD** even if you don't feel ready because you **DREAM BIG**, start small and act. I hope you **BUILD A FOUNDATION** for yourself and your students and you can **BE GRITTY** enough to withstand any storm that comes your way. At the end of the day, I hope you know you gave it your best and when it's time to leave it will be a **GOOD-BYE**. I know you will **MAKE A DIFFERENCE** because as Winnie the Pooh says, "you are braver than you believe, stronger than you seem, smarter than you think and loved more than you know."[9] It's time for you to **TELL YOUR STORY...BECAUSE OF 4!**

TELL YOUR STORY
step-by-step

Your story matters.
Play with ways you can tell your story.

PLAY

Change starts one student at a time, one story at a time. Shadow a
student and identify hacks you might take to impact change.

PRACTICE

Because of 4...Be More!
Name 4 students. Tell your story about them. >AND
YOU!

PURPOSE

Afterword

Many people ask me, "Do you still see the boys?" "Where are they now?" "What about Mrs. G?"

My relationship with Mrs. G has continued to blossom. We moved beyond colleagues to friends. While we don't see each other as often as we would like, we still share inspirational texts or interesting ideas we find with each other. We have been lucky to be able to spend time together with our families and develop a more personal rather than professional relationship. I was blessed to have Mrs. G cheerlead me through this process and push me to the very end. She even agreed to write the forward for the book.

Unfortunately, I have not been so lucky with the boys. First, I lost contact with Michael. By the start of the next school year, Michael had moved with no forwarding information. Jerry and I exchanged a few letters, but then that connection was lost too. Over the next two years I made a few trips to Minnesota. I was able to check in on Larry and Rick during one of those visits. Soon after that, Rick transferred to another school and I lost contact with him.

The boys would be in high school now. I'm not sure where they are or how they are doing. I had hoped for a different outcome. I had hoped to someday watch as they received their diplomas or to send them a college care package. Maybe someday I will still get that chance. This book has given me the opportunity to reconnect with many of my former colleagues and teachers. Perhaps someday it will give me the opportunity for me to reconnect with the four boys too. When I do, I hope we will have an amazing new story to tell.

Bibliography

BECAUSE OF 4...RESOURCE LIST

Lean In

Robbins, M. (2017). *The 5 second rule: The fastest way to change your life*. Savio Republic.

Believe in Miracles

Elrod, H. (2020). *Miracle equation: The two decisions that move your biggest goals from possible, to probable, to... inevitable*. John Murray Learning.

Thirst for Learning

Costa, A. L., & Kallick, B. (2000). *Habits of mind*. Association for Supervision and Curriculum Development.

Keva planks official website. KEVA Planks Official Website. (n.d.). Retrieved July 22, 2022, from https://www.kevaplanks.com/

Peterson, C. (2021). *Super habits: building superpowers with play, practice, and purpose*. https://books.apple.com/us/book/super-habits-ebook/id1585291680

Succeeding with habits of mind. Habits of Mind. (2020, September 21). Retrieved July 22, 2022, from https://habitsofmind.org/succeeding-with-habits-of-mind/

Be in the Moment

Center for mindfulness. UMass Memorial Health. (n.d.). Retrieved July 22, 2022, from https://www.ummhealth.org/center-mindfulness

Davidson, R. (n.d.). *Home*. Center for Healthy Minds. Retrieved July 22, 2022, from https://centerhealthyminds.org/

Harris, D. (2019). *10% Happier: How I tamed the voice in my head, reduced stress without losing my edge, and found self-help that actually works: A true story*. Yellow Kite.

Rechtschaffen, D. J. (2014). *The way of mindful education: Cultivating well-being in teachers and students*. W.W. Norton & Company.

What's Your Word?

Aubin Pictures. (2004). *A Touch of Greatness*. https://itvs.org/films/touch-of-greatness

Ballew, J. (2018, August 29). The Power of Words: Teaching With The Dot and Ish. Retrieved December 15, 2020, from https://www.scholastic.com/teachers/blog-posts/julie-ballew/2017/The-Power-of-Words/

Byrdseed, I. (2022, June 15). *Think like a disciplinarian: Where to start?* Byrdseed. Retrieved July 22, 2022, from https://www.byrdseed.com/thinking-like-a-disciplinarian-in-ela/

Cullum, A. (n.d.). *The geranium on the windowsill just died*. Harlin Quist.

Heath, C., & Heath, D. (2013). *Switch: How to change things when change is hard*. Random House US.

Bibliography

Pan, C. (n.d.). *Myintent project*. MyIntent Project. Retrieved July 22, 2022, from https://myintent.org/

Reynolds, P. H. (2021). *The Dot*. Candlewick Press.

Reynolds, P. (n.d.). *International dot day*. International Dot Day. Retrieved July 22, 2022, from https://www.internationaldotday.org/

It's Playtime!

Brown, B. (2013). *The Gifts of Imperfect Parenting: Raising Children with Courage, Compassion and Connection*. Sounds True.

Brown, S. (2008, May). *Play is more than just fun*. Speech presented at TED. Retrieved December 15, 2020, from https://www.ted.com/talks/stuart_brown_play_is_more_than_just_fun?utm_campaign=tedspread&utm_medium=referral&utm_source=tedcomshare

Carter, C. (2017). *The sweet spot*. Ballantine Books.

Kang, S. K. (2015). *The self-motivated kid: How to raise happy, healthy children who know what they want and go after it (without being told)*. Jeremy P. Tarcher/Penguin.

Little Bits Resource Library. The Complete Littlebits Library of steam and coding lessons. (n.d.). Retrieved July 22, 2022, from https://classroom.littlebits.com/welcome

LittleBits: Electronic Building Kits for Kids. (n.d.). Retrieved December 15, 2020, from https://sphero.com/pages/littlebits

McQuaid, M. (2019, August 06). Can A Question Change Your Life?: Appreciative Inquiry. Retrieved December 16, 2020, from https://www.michellemcquaid.com/can-question-change-life/

Change the World

Cain's Arcade: Our story. Imagination.org. (n.d.). Retrieved July 22, 2022, from https://imagination.org/about-us/our-story/

Juliani, A. J. (n.d.). *Genius hour master course*. Blend Education. Retrieved July 22, 2022, from https://www.blendeducation.org/p/gh

Peterson, C. (2021). IDEAS: A kid's guide to learning about anything. https://books.apple.com/us/book/ideas/id1580840121

Peterson, C. (2022). IDEAS: A simple guide for kids to learn about anything. Explore-IDEAS publishing.

Spencer, J. (2020, October 15). *Join us for the Global Day of Design on May 6th*. John Spencer. Retrieved July 22, 2022, from https://spencerauthor.com/gdd2020/ Original Global Day of Design links no longer available.

Yamada, K. (2021). *What do you do with an idea?* Library Ideas, LLC.

Leap and Lead

Hardy, B. (2019). *Willpower doesn't work: Discover the hidden keys to success*. Piatkus.

Schlechty Center. (n.d.). Retrieved July 22, 2022, from https://www.schlechtycenter.org/

Schlechty, P. C. (2011). *Engaging students: The next level of working on the work*. Jossey-Bass.

3D design methodology. Spring Lake Park Schools. (n.d.). Retrieved July 22, 2022, from

Bibliography

https://www.springlakeparkschools.org/academics/innovation-and-design/3d-methodology

Dream Big

Sanborn, M. (2008).*The Fred Factor*. London: Cornerstone Digital. http://fredfactor.com

KEVA Planks Official Website. (n.d.). Retrieved December 16, 2020, from https://www.kevaplanks.com/

Schlechty Center. (n.d.). Retrieved December 16, 2020, from https://www.schlechtycenter.org/

Build a Foundation

Dweck, C. S. (2017). *Mindset*. Robinson.

Juliani, A. J. (2022). *A Learning Experience to Change Learning*. Innovative Teaching Academy. Retrieved July 22, 2022, from https://innovativeteachingacademy.com/

Be Gritty!

Cole, S. F., Eisner, A., Gregory, M., & Ristuccia, J. (2013). *Helping traumatized children learn*. Massachusetts Advocates for Children.

Duckworth, A. (2019). *Grit*. Vermilion.

KPJR Films. (n.d.). *Paper Tigers*. Retrieved July 22, 2022, from https://kpjrfilms.co/paper-tigers/.

Most Likely to Succeed. (2017). Retrieved July 22, 2022, from https://teddintersmith.com/mltsfilm/.

Stevens, J. E., Godbold, L., Irwin, L., & Paull, S. (2022, July 13). *Aces too high*. Retrieved July 22, 2022, from https://acestoohigh.com/

Good...BYE

Brown, B. (2011, January 3). *The Power of Vulnerability*. Bing. Retrieved July 22, 2022, from https://youtu.be/iCvmsMzlF7o

Elrod, H. (2019). *The miracle morning: The not-so-obvious secret guaranteed to transform your life before 8AM*. Hal Elrod International.

Limited, M. G. (n.d.). *Write a letter to your future self*. FutureMe. Retrieved July 22, 2022, from https://www.futureme.org/

Pausch, R., & Zaslow, J. (2018). *The last lecture*. Hachette Books.

Make a Difference

Greater good in action. (n.d.). Retrieved July 22, 2022, from https://ggia.berkeley.edu/

Helmstetter, K. (2022). *Coffee self-talk 5 minutes a day to start Living your magical life*. Rodale.

Reynolds, M. (2014, March 15). *Teddy Stallard Story*. Makeadifferencemovie.com. Retrieved July 22, 2022, from https://makeadifferencemovie.com/index.php

Seavert, L. (2022). *Love them first - lessons from Lucy Laney Elementary*. Love Them First - Lessons from Lucy Laney Elementary. Retrieved July 22, 2022, from https://www.lovethemfirst.com/

YouTube. (2016, December 8). *The chen miller story - special educational needs teachers*. YouTube. Retrieved July 22, 2022, from https://www.youtube.com/watch?v= G0Lar94iNFM

Tell Your Story

Wagner, T., & Dintersmith, T. (2016). *Most likely to succeed: Preparing our kids for the innovation era*. Scribner.

Dintersmith, T. (2018). *What school could be: Insights and inspiration from Teachers Across America*. Edu21c Foundation.

Scott, M. (2022, July 22). *Scholar, speaker, author*. Manny Scott. Retrieved July 22, 2022, from https://www.mannyscott.com/

Scott, M. V. (2015). *Your next chapter: How to turn the page and create the life of your dreams*. CreateSpace Independent Publishing Platform.

Shadow a student challenge. Stanford d.school. (n.d.). Retrieved July 22, 2022, from https://dschool.stanford.edu/shadow-a-student-k12

Notes

Introduction

1. Paramount home entertainment. (2007). *Freedom Writers* [Film]. United States.
2. Gruwell, E., & Filipović, Z. (2019). *The Freedom Writers Diary: How a teacher and 150 teens used writing to change themselves and the world around them.* Broadway Books.

1. STUDENTS

1. Brown, B. (2019). *Dare to lead: Brave work, tough conversations, whole hearts.* Random House Large Print Publishing.
2. Robbins, M. (2018, December 13). The 5 Second Rule. Retrieved from https://melrobbins.com/blog/the-5-second-rule/

2. MIRACLES

1. Al Michaels. (2020, December 12). Retrieved December 15, 2020, from https://en.wikipedia.org/wiki/Al_Michaels
2. What is Chaos Theory? (n.d.). Retrieved December 15, 2020, from https://fractalfoundation.org/resources/what-is-chaos-theory/
3. Elrod, H. (2019). *The miracle equation.* New York: Random House Large Print.
4. Brown, B. (2019, August 21). What Toni Morrison Taught Me About Parenting. Retrieved from https://brenebrown.com/blog/2019/08/07/what-toni-morrison-taught-me-about-parenting/

3. HABITS

1. Costa, A. L., & Kallick, B. (2000). *Habits of mind.* Alexandria, VA: Association for Supervision and Curriculum Developmen
2. KEVA Planks Official Website. (n.d.). Retrieved December 16, 2020, from https://www.kevaplanks.com/
3. Costa, A. L., & Kallick, B. (2000). *Habits of mind.* Alexandria, VA: Association for Supervision and Curriculum Development.
4. Costa, A. L., & Kallick, B. (2000). *Habits of mind.* Alexandria, VA: Association for Supervision and Curriculum Development.
5. Costa, A. L., & Kallick, B. (2000). *Habits of mind.* Alexandria, VA: Association for Supervision and Curriculum Development. P.16.
6. Wonder Grove Learn Habits of Mind Animations. (n.d.). Retrieved December 15, 2020, from https://wondergrovelearn.net/products/2/1

7. Anderson, J. (2017, October 19). Teacher Resource Library. Retrieved December 15, 2020, from https://habitsofmind.org/resource-library/
8. Anderson, J. (2020, September 21). Succeeding with Habits of Mind. Retrieved December 15, 2020, from https://habitsofmind.org/
9. https://habitsofmind.org/category/free-resources/

4. MINUTES

1. King, M. L., Jr. (n.d.). Martin Luther King, Jr. Quotes. Retrieved December 15, 2020, from https://www.brainyquote.com/quotes/martin_luther_king_jr_106169
2. Little Bits
3. Davidson, R., & Tippet, K. (2019, February 14). Richard Davidson - A Neuroscientist on Love and Learning. Retrieved December 15, 2020, from https://onbeing.org/programs/richard-davidson-a-neuroscientist-on-love-and-learning-feb2019/
4. Rechtschaffen, D. (2014). *The way of mindful education: Cultivating well-being in teachers and students.* New York, NY: W.W. Norton & Company.
5. History of Mindfulness: From East to West and Religion to Science. (2020, September 01). Retrieved December 15, 2020, from https://positivepsychologyprogram.com/history-of-mindfulness/
6. History of Mindfulness: From East to West and Religion to Science. (2020, September 01). Retrieved December 15, 2020, from https://positivepsychologyprogram.com/history-of-mindfulness/
7. Rechtschaffen, D. (2014). *The way of mindful education: Cultivating well-being in teachers and students.* New York, NY: W.W. Norton & Company. P. 26 citing Jacobs, et.al. 2011.
8. Rechtschaffen, D. (2014).Â *The way of mindful education: Cultivating well-being in teachers and students.* New York, NY: W.W. Norton & Company.
9. ADD Mindful Schools
10. Center for Healthy Minds. (n.d.). Retrieved December 15, 2020, from https://centerhealthyminds.org/
11. Harris, D. (2019). *10% happier: How I tamed the voice in my head, reduced stress without losing my edge, and found self-help that actually works -- a true story.* New York: Dey St., an imprint of William Morrow.
12. Harris, D., & Goldstein, J. (n.d.). Mindfulness Meditation. Retrieved December 15, 2020, from https://www.tenpercent.com/
13. Experience Calm. (n.d.). Retrieved December 15, 2020, from https://www.calm.com./
14. Calm Schools Initiative. (n.d.). Retrieved December 15, 2020, from https://www.calm.com/schools

5. SCHOLARS

1. 45 Motivational Robert Kiyosaki Quotes for Success in Life. (n.d.). Retrieved December 15, 2020, from https://www.overallmotivation.com/quotes/robert-kiyosaki-quotes/
2. ADD Switch
3. Cullum, A. (1971). *The geranium on the windowsill just died.* Harlin Quist.

4. Kaplan, S. N. (2014). *Think like a disciplinarian.* Corwin Pres
5. Independent Lens. A TOUCH OF GREATNESS. The Teacher. (n.d.). Retrieved December 15, 2020, from https://www.pbs.org/independentlens/touchofgreatness/teacher.html
6. Pan, C. (n.d.). MyIntent Project. Retrieved December 15, 2020, from https://myintent.org/
7. Dweck, C. S. (2017). *Mindset.* London: Robinson, an imprint of Constable & Robinson.
8. Reynolds, P. (n.d.). Peter H. Reynolds. Retrieved December 15, 2020, from http://www.peterhreynolds.com/
9. Reynolds, P. H. (2021). *The DOT.* S.l.: Candlewick Press.
10. Reynolds, P. (n.d.). Celebrate Creativity, Courage & Collaboration! International Dot Day. Retrieved December 15, 2020, from http://www.thedotclub.org/dotday/
11. Ballew, J. (2018, August 29). The Power of Words: Teaching with The Dot and Ish. Retrieved December 15, 2020, from https://www.scholastic.com/teachers/blog-posts/julie-ballew/2017/The-Power-of-Words/

6. LETTERS

1. Fred Rogers Center. (2018). Retrieved December 15, 2020, from https://www.fredrogerscenter.org/
2. Little Bits: Electronic Building Kits for Kids. (n.d.). Retrieved December 15, 2020, from https://sphero.com/pages/littlebits
3. Carter, C. (2017). *The sweet spot: How to accomplish more by doing less.* New York, NY: Ballantine Books.
4. Brown, S. (2008, May). *Play is more than just fun.* Speech presented at TED. Retrieved December 15, 2020, from https://www.ted.com/talks/stuart_brown_play_is_more_than_just_fun?utm_campaign=tedspread&utm_medium=referral&utm_source=tedcomshare
5. Brown, S. (2008, May). *Play is more than just fun.* Speech presented at TED. Retrieved December 15, 2020, from https://www.ted.com/talks/stuart_brown_play_is_more_than_just_fun?utm_campaign=tedspread&utm_medium=referral&utm_source=tedcomshare
6. Kang, S. K. (2015). *The self-motivated kid: How to raise happy, healthy children who know what they want and go after it (without being told).* New York, NY: Tarcher.
7. Brown, B. (2013). *The Gifts of Imperfect Parenting: Raising Children with Courage, Compassion and Connection.* Sounds True.
8. Building Communities Through Play and Recreation. (n.d.). Retrieved December 16, 2020, from https://www.playcore.com/
9. McQuaid, M. (2019, August 06). Can A Question Change Your Life? Appreciative Inquiry. Retrieved December 16, 2020, from https://www.michellemcquaid.com/can-question-change-life/

7. IDEAS

1. Yamada, K. (2019). *What do you do with an idea?* Compendium.
2. Seuss. (2000). *The Grinch.* Minneapolis, MN: Manhattan Toy.
3. Pruitt, S. (2017, April 07). Here Are 6 Things Albert Einstein Never Said. Retrieved December 16, 2020, from https://www.history.com/news/here-are-6-things-albert-einstein-never-said
4. Eichel, L. (2016, May 24). Experience the MIT motto "Mens et Manus" in upcoming MOOCs. Retrieved December 16, 2020, from https://openlearning.mit.edu/news-events/blog/experience-mit-motto-mens-et-manus-upcoming-moocs
5. Caine's Arcade: A boy's cardboard arcade that inspired the world. (n.d.). Retrieved December 16, 2020, from http://cainesarcade.com/cardboardchallenge/
6. Slpvideo. (2016, June 08). Park Terrace students design cardboard mini-golf course. Retrieved December 16, 2020, from https://www.youtube.com/watch?v=DtacLucuzmg
7. Alveshere, O. (2016, June 17). Park Terrace students build extreme miniature golf course. Retrieved December 16, 2020, from https://www.hometownsource.com/abc_newspapers/news/education/park-terrace-students-build-extreme-miniature-golf-course/article_809980b8-325c-5b03-a7a6-115a30cf071a.html
8. Dewey, J. (2015). *Experience and education.* New York: Free Press.
9. Covadonga, F. (2018, August 08). The Origins of the Maker Movement. Retrieved December 16, 2020, from https://www.bbvaopenmind.com/en/the-origins-of-the-maker-movement/
10. Davis, V. (2014, July 18). How the Maker Movement Is Moving Into Classrooms. Retrieved December 16, 2020, from https://www.edutopia.org/blog/maker-movement-moving-into-classrooms-vicki-davis
11. Juliani, A. (2016, February 08). Genius Hour. Retrieved December 16, 2020, from http://www.geniushour.com/
12. Spencer, J., & Juliani, A. J. (2016).Â *Launch: Using design thinking to boost creativity and bring out the maker in every student.* San Diego, CA: Dave Burgess Consulting.
13. Global Day of Design. (n.d.). Retrieved December 16, 2020, from http://globaldayofdesign.com/. Link no longer available. Please see https://youtu.be/3q5Lgc7AF6M for John Spencer's Global Day of Design explanation.
14. Peterson, C. (2022). IDEAS: A simple guide for kids to learn about anything. Explore-IDEAS publishing.
15. Peterson, C. (2022). *IDEAS: A Simple Guide for Kids to Learn About Anything.* Barrington Hills, IL: Dr. Cheryl Peterson - Explore-IDEAS Publishing.

8. LEADERS

1. Vince Lombardi Quotes. (n.d.). Retrieved December 16, 2020, from https://www.brainyquote.com/quotes/vince_lombardi_130743
2. Hardy, B. (2019). *Willpower doesn't work: Discover the hidden keys to success.* London: Piatkus.
3. Schlechty, P. C. (2011). *Engaging Students: The Next Level of Working on the Work.* Hoboken: John Wiley & Sons.

4. What Is Design Thinking? (2012, July 25). Retrieved December 16, 2020, from https://www.edutopia.org/what-is-design-thinking-for-educators
5. 3D Design Methodology. (n.d.). Retrieved December 16, 2020, from https://www.springlakeparkschools.org/academics/innovation-and-design/3d-methodology

9. PLANS

1. Anderson, J.,(2020, August 26). Spider-Man: 15 Most Iconic Quotes Ever, Ranked. Retrieved December 16, 2020, from https://www.cbr.com/spider-man-most-iconic-quotes-ever-marvel/
2. KEVA Planks Official Website. (n.d.). Retrieved December 16, 2020, from https://www.kevaplanks.com/
3. Sanborn, M. (2008). *The Fred Factor*. London: Cornerstone Digital. http://fredfactor.com
4. Acar, O., Tarakci, M., & VanKnippenberg, D. (2019, November 22). Why Constraints Are Good for Innovation. Retrieved December 16, 2020, from https://hbr.org/2019/11/why-constraints-are-good-for-innovation
5. Schlechty Center. (n.d.). Retrieved December 16, 2020, from https://www.schlechtycenter.org/

10. HOUSES

1. Michael Jordan Quotes (Author of Driven from Within). (n.d.). Retrieved December 16, 2020, from https://www.goodreads.com/author/quotes/16823.Michael_Jordan
2. KEVA Planks Official Website. (n.d.). Retrieved December 16, 2020, from https://www.kevaplanks.com/
3. Mackinnon, M., & Ligi, R. (2020). *The gingerbread man*. Tulsa, OK: EDC Publishing.
4. Dweck, C. S. (2017). *Mindset*. London: Robinson, an imprint of Constable & Robinson.
5. Costa, A. L., & Kallick, B. (2000). *Habits of mind*. Alexandria, VA: Association for Supervision and Curriculum Development.
6. Juliani, A. (n.d.). The Innovative Teaching Academy. Retrieved December 17, 2020, from http://innovativeteachingacademy.org/

11. WEEKS

1. Tennyson, A. (n.d.). A quote from In Memoriam. Retrieved December 17, 2020, from https://www.goodreads.com/quotes/1946-tis-better-to-have-loved-and-lost-than-never-to
2. Dintersmith, T. (2020, March 25). Most Likely To Succeed. Retrieved December 17, 2020, from http://www.mltsfilm.org/
3. Paper Tigers. (2016, April 07). Retrieved December 17, 2020, from https://kpjr-films.co/paper-tigers/
4. Duckworth, A. (2019). *Grit*. London: Vermilion. doi:https://angeladuckworth.com

5. Anthony, B. (n.d.). Grit Necklace. Retrieved December 17, 2020, from https://www.bryananthonys.com/collections/womens-necklaces/products/grit-baroque-pearl-necklace

6. Duckworth, A. (n.d.). Grit Scale. Retrieved December 17, 2020, from https://angeladuckworth.com/grit-scale/

7. About the CDC-Kaiser Ace Study |Violence prevention|injury Center|CDC. (2021, April 06). Retrieved July 3, 2022, from https://www.cdc.gov/violenceprevention/aces/about.html

8. Got your Aces Score? (n.d.). Retrieved December 16, 2020, from https://acestoohigh.com/got-your-ace-score/

9. What is Early Childhood Development? A Guide to Brain Development. (2019, March 21). Retrieved December 17, 2020, from https://developingchild.harvard.edu/resources/five-numbers-to-remember-about-early-childhood-development/

10. TLPI Publications - Helping Traumatized Children Learn. (2020, July 04). Retrieved December 17, 2020, from https://traumasensitiveschools.org/tlpi-publications/

11. Economy, P. (2016, January 15). 15 Disney Quotes That Will Inspire Your Success. Retrieved December 17, 2020, from https://www.inc.com/peter-economy/15-motivating-disney-quotes-that-will-inspire-your-success.html

12. GOOD-BYES

1. Milne, A. (n.d.). A quote from The Complete Tales of Winnie-the-Pooh. Retrieved December 17, 2020, from https://www.goodreads.com/quotes/7547425-how-lucky-am-i-to-have-something-that-makes-saying

2. Brown, B. (2011, January 3). The Power of Vulnerability. Retrieved December 17, 2020, from https://www.bing.com/videos/search?q=brene+brown+vulnerability+ted+talk

3. Pausch, R. (2007, December 20). Randy Pausch Last Lecture: Achieving Your Childhood Dreams. Retrieved December 17, 2020, from https://www.youtube.com/watch?v=ji5_MqicxSo

4. Elrod, H. (2018). *The miracle morning: The not-so-obvious secret guaranteed to transform your life before 8AM*. Place of publication not identified: Hal Elrod International.

5. FutureMe Labs. (n.d.). Write a Letter to your Future Self. Retrieved December 17, 2020, from https://www.futureme.org/

13. WORDS

1. Brown, B. (n.d.). Brene Brown Quotes On Vulnerability, Courage, Love, Shame, Connection. Retrieved December 17, 2020, from https://www.overallmotivation.com/quotes/brene-brown-quotes/

2. Taylor, J., & Taylor, J. (1978). *The Bible*. Rutland: Printed by Fay & Davison.

3. Reynolds, M. (n.d.). The Teddy Stallard Story. Retrieved December 17, 2020, from https://www.makeadifferencemovie.com/index.php

4. Love Them First - Lessons from Lucy Laney Elementary. (n.d.). Retrieved December 17, 2020, from https://www.lovethemfirst.com/

5. Helmstetter, K. (2020). *Coffee self-talk: 5 minutes a day to start Living your magical life.* Green Butterfly Press.
6. Loving-Kindness Meditation (Greater Good in Action). (n.d.). Retrieved December 17, 2020, from https://ggia.berkeley.edu/practice/loving_kindness_meditation
7. Miller, C. (2016, December 08). The Chen Miller Story - Special Educational Needs Teachers. Retrieved December 17, 2020, from https://www.youtube.com/watch?v=G0Lar94iNFM
8. Milne, A. (n.d.). A quote from Winnie the Pooh Library. Retrieved December 17, 2020, from https://www.goodreads.com/quotes/6659295-you-are-braver-than-you-believe-stronger-than-you-seem
9. Milne, A. (n.d.). A quote from Winnie the Pooh Library. Retrieved December 17, 2020, from https://www.goodreads.com/quotes/6659295-you-are-braver-than-you-believe-stronger-than-you-seem

14. PROMISES

1. Songfacts. (n.d.). Lyrics for closing time by Semisonic - Songfacts. Retrieved October 20, 2022, from https://www.songfacts.com/lyrics/semisonic/closing-time
2. Dintersmith, T. (2020, March 25). Most Likely To Succeed. Retrieved December 17, 2020, from https://teddintersmith.com/mltsfilm/
3. Dintersmith, T. (2018). *What school could be: Insights and inspiration from teachers across America.* Boston: Edu21c Foundation.
4. Scott, M. (2020, December 16). Scholar, Speaker, Author. Retrieved December 17, 2020, from https://www.mannyscott.com/
5. *Freedom writers.* [Motion picture on DVD]. (2007). Paramount.
6. Scott, M. (2022, July 03). Manuel Scott, ph.D.. Retrieved July 3, 2022, from https://www.mannyscott.com/meet-manny
7. Shadow a Student Challenge. (n.d.). Retrieved December 17, 2020, from http://shadowastudent.org/
8. Dintersmith, T. (2018). *What school could be: Insights and inspiration from teachers across America.* Boston: Edu21c Foundation.
9. Milne, A. (n.d.). A quote from Winnie the Pooh Library. Retrieved December 17, 2020, from https://www.goodreads.com/quotes/6659295-you-are-braver-than-you-believe-stronger-than-you-seem

Acknowledgments

This book would not have been possible without the help and support of many people. There are so many people throughout my life who have supported me, taught me and made this book possible. My parents, Walt and Diane, my husband, Darrin, and my kids, Elena and Ben, have provided constant support and inspiration. My whole extended family including my brother, cousins, aunts and uncles and grandparents have always encouraged me. When I got married, Grandma Wille gave me a savings bond and told me to use it for my education. 30 years later it doubled in value and provided the funds for this book. But her biggest investment was the time she spent with me. She took me on trips, baked, let the cousins have sleep overs and put on plays with the best dress-up clothes ever, and kept a card with gold stars for when I achieved something in school. This investment of time and love inspired me and formed my foundation as a parent and teacher.

Countless teachers, parents and coaches have inspired me with their example, challenged my thinking and helped me to become a better teacher. While I can't possibly thank all of them, there are a few who I need to recognize. My GT team, Marianne Paulos, Sarah Nimlos, Jean Nolby, Angel Pearson, Sue Feigal-Hitch and Pam McDonald were my colleagues and mentors. Hope Rahn, Mike Callahan, and Kim Fehringer pushed me to work harder, learn more and grow in many ways and supported me in the role of gifted specialist and coordinator. Desiree Gillis and Laurie Roberts encouraged me as a writer and read my first drafts. Zach Roberts reminded me why it's so important to get this right. Dana Hagerman, who has been my friend since preschool, and Leslee Dirnberger, a new friend in the homeschooling world, pushed me to think critically and escaped with me for writing retreats. Mrs. Wright, Mrs. Czupeck, Ms. Hart, Miss Murphy, Mr. Block, and Mr. Loewe are just a few of the teachers who taught me and inspired me to be teacher. In addition, Dr. Alice Maday, a colleague and mentor at the University of Minnesota, and Dr. Darlene Hoffman, my advisor at Millikin University, set the foundation for my interest in play, practice and purpose. Ms. Andersson and Miss Annie showed me the strengths in my own children and how to reach a struggling student by building relationships. So many of my colleagues have inspired me through the years and their examples have made me a better teacher. I know I will miss some in this list, but I have to recognize Laura Ugo-Ross, Lindsay Peterson, Amy Reiland, Alicia Koberstein, Lindsay Johnson, Jodianne Coler, Amanda West, Curtis Horton, Jan Burda, Kilee Christnagel, Jenna Eaton, Melissa Gustafson, Ellen Western, Michelle Wollney, Lauren Liang and Melissa Scherkenbach. Thank you. Whether you sat with me in grad school or worked beside me in schools. I am a better teacher because of you.

My cousin, Laura Haver, inspired me with her coaching and has helped me continue to become more and develop my skills as a writer. The Author Moms group she started has been a place to learn, share and grow as a writer and a mom. Special thanks to everyone in the group for sharing your stories, expertise and encouraging big dreams. I also have to thank her parents Lynn and Rick Malone for giving me an amazing retreat in San Diego and for helping with editing.

Writing requires a routine and a place to write. I could not have made it without my dogs, Pepper and Tinker Bell, who kept me company and reminded me to get up and smell the roses. My dog walking team of neighbors, the DOCO: Anne, Stephanie, Deb, Rudy & Tracy, encouraged me every morning. I also have to thank Daily Projects for giving me a place to sit and write and delicious coffee to keep me going. Thanks to Ewa I could focus on writing and have a clean spot to work, and truly understand what it means to have grit.

While four students may have been the catalyst for this story, every student I have ever worked with from Decatur Public Schools, Ridge Central, Cedar Rapids Public Schools, Churchill, Spring Lake Park Schools, Learning Tree and Liberty are in some way part of this story. I hope I taught them and inspired them as much as they have inspired me.

Hal Elrod and A.J. Juliani, while I don't know you, your work has had a huge impact on me and helped me develop the skills, discipline and direction I needed to become a writer and tell this story.

I believe this story was given to me as an answer to a prayer. I thank God for this experience and giving me the nudge and inspiration I needed to write it. My sisters in Christ - Pam, Carla, Carol, Cheri, Diane, Jena, Kristen, Laurie, Nikki, Sue, and Tammy - Thank you for your prayers, encouragement, love and support.

While writers usually do the cover last, it was one of the first things I did. As I was working on my first draft, I was connected to Mackenzie Murray. In our first consult, Mackenzie was excited about my story and agreed to do the cover and later the sketch of the four boys. Looking at this cover and imagining my book completed has helped me to continue working on it. Thank you Mackenzie for putting a cover on my vision and capturing my favorite memory of the boys in their lab coats.

Getting my story out to the world has been one of my biggest challenges. It's one thing to write a book, but it's a whole different skill set and mental challenge to release it out to the world. I can't thank Pam Zeidman enough for her encouragement, pushing, and skills in social media for helping me release this story. Her assistant Savannah used her creativity and skill to turn my words into beautiful posts. Thanks also to Aaron Gang for capturing author images for the book and branding and helping my face light up.

Finally, last but not least, Rick, Michael, Jerry, Larry, and Mrs. G. Thank you for teaching me the importance of play, practice and purpose and giving me a story to tell.

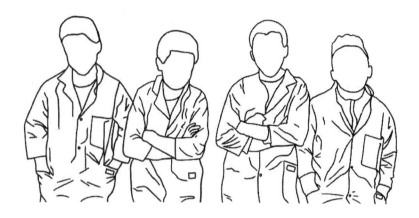

About the Author

Cheryl Peterson, Ph.D. is a mom, teacher, coach and writer. This is Dr. Peterson's first book. Because of four young students, she was inspired to be more. She studied elementary education at Millikin University and then spent nearly 20 years in public education teaching at various grade levels, and working as an instructional coach and gifted coordinator. She has also supervised student teachers at The University of Iowa where she received her Masters Degree in Educational Psychology. She supervised student teachers, conducted research and served as an instructor for preservice teachers at The University of Minnesota where she received her Doctorate in Curriculum and Instruction. With her extensive background in gifted education she has taught as an adjunct professor at Hamline University for six years. She blogs regularly about her experience as a mother, writer, educator and hobby farmer. Since COVID-19 she has utilized her experience to support families and students through tutoring, coaching and teaching a variety of courses in homeschool co-ops. She lives with her husband, children, dog, cats, chickens and horses in Illinois.

www.drcherylpeterson.com

facebook.com/DrCherylPeterson

twitter.com/drcherylpeters1

instagram.com/drcherylpeterson

linkedin.com/in/drcherylpeterson

Also by Cheryl Peterson, Ph.D.

Because of 4 Step-by-Step Workbook Reflection Guide

IDEAS: A Simple Guide for Kids to Learn About Anything

Discover my latest projects and connect with me at

https://linktr.ee/dr.cherylpeterson

Made in the USA
Middletown, DE
24 October 2022

13417520R00115